the ^new Smart Approach to

window decor

CREATIVE HOMEOWNER®, Upper Saddle River, New Jersey

VP/Editorial Director: Timothy O. Bakke
Production Manager: Kimberly H. Vivas

Senior Editor, Decorating: Kathie Robitz
Assistant Editor/Photo Researcher: Jennifer Ramcke
Editorial Assistant: Jennifer Doolittle
Senior Designer: Glee Barre
Illustrator: Barbara Griffel
Templates Illustrator: Tina Basile

Cover Design/Front Cover Photography: John Parsekian/CH; curtain courtesy of Country Curtains

Back Cover Photography: (clockwise from left) Jessie Walker, Phillip Ennis, Mark Lohman

Printed in the United States of America

Current Printing (last digit)
1 0 9 8 7 6 5 4 3 2

The New Smart Approach To Window Decor
Library of Congress Catalog Card Number: 2003112928
ISBN: 1-58011-171-8

CREATIVE HOMEOWNER®
A Division of Federal Marketing Corp.
24 Park Way
Upper Saddle River, NJ 07458
www.creativehomeowner.com

ACKNOWLEDGMENTS

Sincere thanks to all of those who generously offered their assistance, especially the staffs at Windows of Montclair and Country Curtains as well as the American Society of Interior Designers (ASID). Recognition must also go to Anne Marie Soto for her contribution. On a personal note, a special thank you to Dolores and John Elliott for their unfailing support.

CONTENTS

INTRODUCTION

Selecting the right window treatment can be confusing. There are so many things to consider: the architecture of the window, the style of the room, your lifestyle and budget, and how you want the window treatment to look and function. And like any other aspect of good design, dressing a window takes a concentrated effort to get it right. That's how *The New Smart Approach to Window Decor* can help.

By presenting a wide range of window-treatment types and styles, the book provides lots of ideas that can inspire your own design. But more than that, *The New Smart Approach to Window Decor* walks you through the decision-making process, step by step. It helps you to see the "big picture" by first analyzing the structure of the window and its place within the architecture, then showing you how to take that information and study it alongside the other decorative elements of your home. Once you've mastered that, you'll be ready to tackle the questions of lifestyle and budget, which should help you decide whether or not to go the custom route. "Smart Tips" scattered throughout the book offer handy decorator advice, too.

Whichever you choose, custom window treatments or ready-made ones, you'll find the chapters that explore the various types of coverings—curtains and draperies; shades, blinds, and shutters; and cornices, valances, and swags—insightful, particularly when they are combined with the advice for choosing a fabric. If you're looking for a way to add flair to your design, you'll find that the discussion of the various types of decorative embellishments will show you how to add rich details. When

you're ready to install your new window treatment, Chapter 10, "Designer Hardware," starting on page 148, will explain how to select the right type of mounting device.

Some types of windows are challenging to dress because of their size, shape, or location. Chapter 11, "Problem Solving," which begins on page 160, offers solutions to many of the most common problems that homeowners face when challenged with an awkward window placement. If you're handy with sewing projects, you'll find instructions for creating your own curtains, swags, and embellishments in Chapter 12, "Curtains You Can Make," beginning on page 176.

Finally, if you want to play with a few different looks before making up your mind, consult the Appendix on page 186. Scaled versions of various window types and numerous window-treatment styles let you try out a variety of designs so that you can see how they may look in your home. Consult the "Resource Guide," on page 200, for convenient retail information and design sources.

The New Smart Approach to Window Decor should make choosing a window treatment easy and creative—no more worrying about costly mistakes. Take it along when you're shopping or consulting a professional designer.

Left: A balloon valance fashioned from a vibrant fabric adds a soft note to a pair of architecturally strong windows.

Below: Fabric can be installed to emphasize the shape of a pretty bay window.

Opposite: Easy elegance can be achieved simply by draping soft fabric over a good-looking rod.

PERSONALITY AND PRACTICALITY

FORM FOLLOWS FUNCTION ■ THE PRACTICAL ROLE OF WINDOW TREATMENTS

Selecting a window treatment provides you with a terrific opportunity for making changes that can affect how you use a room, your level of comfort or sense of well being when you are in the room, and the visual appeal or success of the overall decor. Plus a window treatment provides all of this for what is often a relatively affordable investment.

When you think of the important role a window treatment plays in your decorating plans, consider a number of factors. Do you need a way to control sunlight and glare? Can you use the window treatment to limit heat gain during the summer or heat loss during the winter? Do you want to obscure an undesirable view? Are you looking for a way to create privacy? Can you use a window treatment to modify or enhance the architectural elements of the space? Can you use it to set a mood, establish a style, or bring color, pattern, and texture into a room?

Of course, the right window treatment can do any of these things. But it can also establish or underscore a decorative style, whether it is contemporary, traditional, country, or period. On a large window or one that is situated prominently, the right dressing can also create a focal point in a space that lacks this important visual anchor.

FORM FOLLOWS FUNCTION

Today, there is a wide selection of window treatments and materials to address any or all of these concerns. Because conditions of light, heat, and lifestyle dictate changes over the course of the day or even from season to season, it's wise to select a style that is easily adjustable. For example, natural light that streams over your shoulder, while you sit in a chair with your back to the window, is lovely for reading a book. However, if you're working at a computer that is in the direct path of harsh sunlight, the glare on the monitor caused by the sun's reflection will make it difficult to read what's on the screen and may strain your eyes. A window covering that can be lowered or closed at will allows you to enjoy natural light when you want it or close it out when you don't.

Before getting started on your window-decor project, go over the following steps to make sure that you're contemplating a window treatment that does the job you need it to do.

SMART steps

ONE Consider ventilation and airflow. Sometimes you'll want to open your windows to let in fresh air and release indoor pollutants. On occasion, you may prefer a natural breeze to an air conditioner. So choose a covering that won't impede the flow of air into the room. On the other hand, if the windows are a source for draughts or heat collection, consider specially insulated curtains that can cut down on these problems and may even save you the cost of replacing old windows.

TWO Examine the sight lines. What is the first thing you see when you enter a room? In most cases, it is the windows. Can you see them from outside the entry? You know what they say about first impressions, so use the window treatments to make an immediate style statement.

Left: A matchstick shade can be raised or lowered to filter light at this desk. Here, it also complements the bamboo furnishings.

Opposite: Pretty balloon shades enhance the shape and appearance of this window bay when viewed from inside and outside of the house.

THREE Look out, look in. Do you want to take in the view? Then, you may want minimal window dressing. But what about privacy? You may feel as if you're living in a fishbowl, especially at night when the interior of the house is lit, unless your property is secluded. A treatment that's adjustable, such as curtains, shades, or blinds that open and close easily, is the solution. But don't ignore the way your window treatment looks from the outside. Choose a style that suits the overall style of your home.

FOUR Observe the architecture. The window treatment you choose is the bridge from window to wall. What you select should blend harmoniously with the architecture and the home's interior design.

If there is a flaw in the design of the space, you can some-times compensate for it with window decor. A treatment can add character that may be lacking or camouflage problems with scale and proportion.

FIVE: Look at the room's general decor. Does it appear tired, dated, or simply unfinished? Consider how new window treatments can put a fresh face on the room.

Above: **Today's** new windows can be large and window-treatment materials lightweight without compromising com-fort, thanks to improved insulated glass.

SMARTtip   Operating the Window

Consider the way a window opens and closes before choosing a window treatment. Double-hung windows pose the fewest problems. Casement windows and French doors that swing into a room require a design that will not obstruct of their paths of operation.

THE PRACTICAL ROLE OF A WINDOW TREATMENT

When you imagine heavy, multi-layered fabric covering a window, it's usually in a period- or historic-design context. (Although lighter-weight versions are popular in traditional homes, today.) Textiles, such as lined wool, damask, silk, brocade, velvet, and tapestries, provided much-needed insulation against extreme temperatures in an era without the luxuries of double-glazed glass, central heating, and air conditioning. Though insulation is often a factor in choosing a window treatment, ventilation and controlling natural light are more common concerns, nowadays.

Any room with an eastern orientation is subject to strong morning light, a consideration acutely important in a bedroom, for example. A room with windows facing west gets strong light in the afternoon; however, if you don't ordinarily use the room at this time of day, you may not care.

North-facing rooms, because they receive no direct sunlight, get chilly, especially during the winter. This makes a good case for insulated window treatments. Spaces with a southern exposure receive the most natural light; during the summer months or in a warm climate, these rooms can get too hot. The right window covering can abate some of the heat buildup. Think about when and where you're most likely

Opposite: You can have the best of both worlds by pairing an stylish permanent treatment, such as this swag-and-jabot design, with a practical adjustable blind.

Above: Room-darkening shades, made from fade-resistant fabric that won't admit light, can be pulled up or down during the day, according to how you want to control the sunlight.

to be affected by natural light and whether you need a means to control it.

The rays of the sun also affect furnishings, so when choosing your window treatment, keep this in mind, as well. Delicate fabrics, wallcoverings, even wood finishes can be harmed by continuous direct exposure to strong natural light. Translucent fabric panels, once called "glass curtains," are often combined with draperies to filter sunlight.

Curtains and Drapery. Loosely hung fabric or panels that are attached to the window frame or sash offer some control over both light and privacy. The level depends on how many layers are installed and whether or not the fabric is

lined. Sheer fabrics allow the transmission of light and don't obscure the view to the outdoors. Sometimes curtains and drapery are not adjustable; they have to be installed with a rod system or rings that allow you to open or close the panels to efficiently control light and privacy.

Shades, Blinds, and Shutters. All three of these treatments are usually fully adjustable and offer complete light and priva-

cy control. Each comes in a multitude of styles, and they can be installed alone or paired with curtains or drapery.

A window treatment can pull together an entire room, often unifying a design of disparate parts. It can change the style or ambiance from casual to formal or from sterile to romantic. New curtains can punch up, tone down, or blend into a color scheme, adding pattern and texture.

Opposite: Gorgeous fabric, trimming, and styling add appropriate drama to a corner of a formal room with lots of classic architectural details.

Above: A simple, understated white louvered shutter adds architectural interest to an undistinguished window in a small room. Here, it also controls light in this sunny bedroom.

Opposite: A lively partnership of prints, borrowed from the banquette and chair cushions, makes up a darling valance in a cheerful breakfast nook.

a gallery of smart ideas

1 An elegant scalloped edging and tassels coordinate a roller shade with a formal curtain and valance.

2 Billowing balloon shades soften the angles of this window bay.

3 A simple floral valance frames a garden view.

4 Layers of fabric add drama to a nondescript window.

5 Charming café curtains and a matching valance suit a country decor.

6 A scarf valance and panels dress up this window without hiding its handsome architecture.

7 Panels that move easily across a rod enhance these French doors.

8 Perfectly plain roller shades are unobtrisively practical in a simple setting.

CHAPTER 2

WINDOW TYPES

WINDOW CLASSIFICATIONS ■ LOOKING AT YOUR WINDOWS ■ SCALE AND PROPORTION ■ LINE ■ BALANCE HARMONY AND RHYTHM

Windows are important architectural elements. The more common types of windows, such as double-hung and casement units, may act as plain backdrops for window dressings. But specialty windows are often associated with a particular architectural style. Compare a triangular window with a Palladian one, for instance. The geometric shape of a triangular window has a modern sensibility, whereas the classic Palladian-style window is considered traditional.

When choosing a treatment, it is not enough to only look at the type and style of the window. You should examine how the window relates to the space around it—its visual weight. Is it a new fixed window in a room with a vintage fireplace and classical moldings? A window can sometimes go against all of the other decorative cues in the room. By assessing its style, you can coordinate the window with the space's decor. Is it a horizontal picture window in a room with low ceilings? This is a problem of proportion. Understanding proportion—and other decorating basics such as scale, balance, line, harmony, and rhythm—will help you to choose a treatment that looks good and functions properly within the context of the room. This chapter will give you all of the information you need to identify and assess your window's style.

WINDOW CLASSIFICATIONS

If you are considering replacing a window, learn about the various types. A fixed window cannot be opened and is often used with an operable window. A double-hung window is the most common of the operable types: it has two sash that move up and down, which means that only half of the window can be completely open at one time. A casement window is hinged vertically to swing in or out. A jalousie window has horizontal slats or narrow strips of

glass that are opened louver-like by a crank. A sliding window or glass door has top and bottom tracks on which the sash moves sideways.

You should also explore the various architectural styles of windows, which often influence your decor. A group of three windows with an arch over the center unit is the classical makeup of a Palladian window. Some variations have three arches (one large, two small) or one fanlight-style arch over the three windows. This classical window

Oppositet: Here you can see how the lattice design on the cornice was inspired by the muntins (the strips that divide the panes).

Right: Flouncy balloon shades and the scalloped hemline of the curtain valances soften a sharp corner with narrow windows.

tends to visually dominate a room, so it is logical as a focal point.

A picture window is made up of one large fixed window, often flanked by two casement or double-hung units. As the name describes, a picture window is for framing dramatic views. Like a Palladian or a picture window, a bay window is also composed of three parts. The difference is that the windows are set at an angle to each other, creating an alcove, or bay. A curved version of this window is called a bow window. A large bay with a window adds about 4 feet of extra space to a room where you can situate a chair or a small dining table.

A clerestory window is made of a strip of small, horizontal panes set high on a wall, near the ceiling. This window is often used in spaces where natural light is desirable but privacy must also be maintained.

There are also a variety of special small window shapes that are almost strictly decorative. These windows are used independently or in combination with the standard types. An elliptical or arched window is often placed above double-hung or fixed windows, but it can also be used alone in situations where a larger unit won't fit, such as in a dormer or a small bathroom. An oval (or cameo) window and a circular window are used in much the same way; both are sometimes located on narrow staircase landings to add light. For a more modern shape, a triangular window or a trapezoidal window is often paired with a large fixed window—a combination known as a cathedral window.

LOOKING AT YOUR WINDOWS

Now that you've established the type of window you have, begin by examining how it relates to other elements in the room. Check how the window and the treatment coordinate. Look at the space itself—is there a prominent architectural style to the room? Also consider the size of the window and how it relates to the space. To get you started, here are some easy steps to follow.

ONE Compare the style of your window with the treatment you're considering. What kind of architectural detail does the window have or lack that you can cover up or enhance? Always remember that decorating and architectural styles are linked, not necessarily in the strictest sense, but there should be a relationship between the two. Heavy brocade panels paired with formal swags will appear out of place in a country parlor. In the same way, ruffled calico curtains strike the wrong note in a room that is streamlined and contemporary.

TWO Consider the size of the window. Particularly in older homes, windows are often too small, even for modest-sized rooms. Sometimes that's just because glass was expensive, so the windows were kept small. But many older houses also had no central heating at the time they were built, so the architect or builder used the same solution to avoid problems with heat loss. As homes were heated more efficiently and technologically advanced glazes were developed, window sizes grew larger. If your windows are small, you can create a more harmonious balance between the window size and the room with the right treatment and installation. For a short window, install the rod above the trim or just below the ceiling line. Hang extra-long panels, and let them puddle. On the window that isn't wide enough for the wall, extend the window treatment beyond the frame on each side of the opening.

Some windows have the opposite problem—they're so large that they overwhelm the entire space. In this case, you can tone down the scale by keeping the look simple. If a window is too tall, don't use long panels. Break up the length by dressing the top of the window with a valance or a swag that's different from the rest of the design. When windows in a room are different sizes, de-emphasize the difference with curtains that are all the same length. Don't pile

Opposite: A lot of contemporary architecture features expansive windows. Window treatments should be selected to let in as much light as possible.

Above: The stack-back position of curtains and draperies that are installed around a slider door opening should accommodate furniture to either side of the door.

Right: Beautiful windows should be seen. The color and pattern of this fabric attracts the eye up to the handsome arch of these Palladian-style windows without covering them.

on several layers, and avoid heavily patterned fabrics. (For more information on working with problem windows, see Chapter 11, "Problem Solving," page 160.)

THREE Take note of how a window functions. Does the window open inward or outward? Does it slide on a track? Where is the handle for the crank located? These small—and seemingly obvious—details can limit your window-covering choices. For instance, shutters may impede

Opposite: Floor-length curtains hanging from a single pole that has been installed near the ceiling make a pair of modest-size double-hung windows appear taller and wider.

Below: Architecturally speaking, casement windows are usually contemporary in style, but this formal window treatment gives them a traditional look.

Left: A classic arch window, sometimes called a "sunburst window," is beautiful and should remain uncovered if possible. Beneath it, fabric is draped uniformly over a pole.

inward-opening windows. Billowing curtains may get caught in the tracks of sliding glass doors. The crank handle on jalousie windows may interfere with blinds or shades. Knowing these limitations and conditions can help you choose the most practical treatment.

SCALE AND PROPORTION

Dressing a window is not always as simple as hanging up attractive curtains. A window covering should be in proportion to the window and the room. If an element is not the right size—let's say, it has a rosette that's too small or an overly long valance—it throws off the entire effect of the treatment. The small rosette will be distracting rather than impressive; the long valance will make the window look squat and will make the room seem smaller. To plan a well-balanced window covering, there are several fundamental

principles relating to space that you should understand. These principles include scale, proportion, line, balance, harmony, and rhythm.

Scale and proportion work hand in hand. In decorating, *scale* simply refers to the size of something as it relates to the size of everything else, including people and the space itself. *Proportion* refers to the relationship of parts or objects to one another based on size—the size of the window is in proportion to the size of the room, for example. Good scale is achieved when all of the parts are proportionately correct relative to each other, as well as to the whole. If you are mixing patterns in an arrangement, for instance, you might want to balance a curtain made from a large-patterned fabric with a lining that has been made using a medium-scale design; then use a small-print fabric for an accent, such as a border.

Occasionally, a window treatment turns out to be too large or too small for its location. Careful planning and a deliberate effort will help you to avoid this and to achieve good proportion in the window covering itself, as well as its completed effect in the room. One way to test your ideas is to make a measured drawing of the window. (For more information on measuring windows, see Chapter 12, "Curtains You Can Make," page 176.) Then you can take your time and experiment with different arrangements on paper until something looks right.

Left: Two small windows are transfomed by an illusion of grander proportions simply because the curtains are very full and have been installed from floor to ceiling. Visual tricks can often compensate for a room's shortcomings.

LINE

Next to consider is *line*. Simply put, line defines space. Two-dimensional space consists of flat surfaces, such as walls, floors, and windows, that are formed by intersecting lines. Adding depth, or volume, to a flat surface creates three-dimensional space—a house or a room, for example. However, lines also suggest various qualities:

■ **Vertical lines** imply strength, dignity, and formality. Imagine how impressive a pair of tall, narrow windows flanking a fireplace would look.

■ **Horizontal lines,** such as a row of clerestory windows or even a cornice across a picture window, on the other hand, convey relaxation and security.

■ **Diagonal lines,** such as a triangular or trapezoidal window, express motion, transition, and change.

■ **Curved lines,** like those of an arched window or the shape of a swag, denote softness and sensuality.

Windows and their coverings are a way to incorporate a variety of lines into a room's design. Most modern rooms are rectilinear. Window dressings can help relieve the repetition of squares and rectangles inherent in the architecture. Tieback draperies or fan shades can introduce a few curves and make the space more interesting.

BALANCE, HARMONY, RHYTHM

Balance keeps the relationships between the parts of a room natural and comfortable to the eye. For instance, two windows side by side on a wall with matching floor-length curtains will look appropriate in a room, whereas the same setting with a sill-length curtain on one window and a floor-length curtain on the other will seem awkward and out of balance. Balanced relationships can be either symmetrical or asymmetrical. A swag with two matching cascade jabots is a good example of a symmetrical design. Picture that same swag with a long jabot on just one side, and you have an example of an asymmetrical design.

Harmony is achieved by coordinating all of the elements within one scheme or motif. Matching styles, colors, and patterns are good examples.

Rhythm refers to repeated patterns, which add movement and interest. So while harmony pulls a treatment together, rhythm moves the eye. The key to creating good harmony and rhythm is balance.

Designers always suggest introducing one or two contrasting elements to a room's design. Some little surprise, such as an unexpected splash of contrasting color, can really perk up a boring design. You can apply this to a window treatment. For example, think about using a contrasting curtain liner or a band of color, beads, or fringe around the edges of a plain curtain panel to add pizzazz.

Above: There is a lot going on here, from the heavily patterned rug and the cushion fabrics to the deep tones of the wood and leather upholstery. That didn't stop the designer from carrying the opulent theme to the windows. But, united by the wall's color, all of the elements appear harmonious.

1 Simple curtains that are swept back provide a classic frame for a window.

2 Repeating a style throughout different areas in an open plan creates a unified look.

3 Installing the rod just below the top portion of the window trim allows this architectural detail to remain visible.

4 A repeating valance draws the eye around the room.

5 Swags that hang near the ceiling give the small windows over the tub the same visual weight as the French doors.

6 An attractive London shade serves with style, but without taking up much space on a small wall behind a bed.

a gallery

of smart ideas

CHAPTER 3

PLANNING YOUR DESIGN

ASSESSING STYLE NEEDS ▦
COLOR ▦ PATTERN ▦ TEXTURE ▦
PULLING IT ALL TOGETHER

Why does something as simple as selecting a curtain or a blind fluster an ordinarily decisive person? Perhaps it's because there are too many options. However, a good general rule for starters is to match the style of the window treatment to the style of the room. If the architecture is traditional, the curtains should be equally classical in their construction and fabric. Modern rooms call for up-to-date treatments. You can always bend the rules. The trick is knowing when and when not to play against type. For success, consult a professional about this.

Color, pattern, and texture are great tools for coordinating window treatments with the rest of the design elements in a room. Use them to make windows stand out or blend into the background. Color, pattern, and texture can alter a window spatially, too, making it seem smaller or larger, depending on the scale of the design and the intensity of the hue. The most subtle of the three elements, texture, adds complexity by incorporating fabrics with matte, coarse, smooth, or glossy weaves. To try out all of these pieces, make a designer's sample board. This is an efficient way to combine—and edit out—fabrics in different colors, patterns, and textures. Doing this will give you the confidence that what you are envisioning will accomplish your goals.

ASSESSING STYLE NEEDS

What do you want to achieve with your window treatment? It can enhance a space's good qualities by framing a beautiful view or incorporating color, pattern, and texture into the room. It can enliven a nondescript interior, serve as a focal point, or visually improve the room's spatial relationship. A window treatment is also an important way to establish a style. The wrong window dressing can throw off the entire decorating scheme. For example, ruffled calico curtains would look odd in a modern chrome-and-leather setting. To help you make a decision about your window-treatment needs, follow these steps.

 SMART steps

ONE Take note of the room's function. In the previous two chapters, you looked at the window's function in a room—in terms of light control and privacy, as well as how its architectural style influences a space. Now look at the use of the room itself. It often dictates the type of window treatment that is needed. In a dining room—a space used mostly for entertaining—a window dressing may be chosen for its dramatic effect. A bedroom with a window facing the street may need a cover-up for privacy. To cut the glare on a desk, a study may require shades or shutters. The purpose of a room may limit your window-covering choices.

TWO Establish the style of the room. Is it traditional? Contemporary? Period? Eclectic? Country? Window treatments set the tone of a room, enhancing the ambiance. Most types of treatments conjure an image of a certain style. Puddled drapery with a cornice is usually considered traditional; vertical blinds in a textured finish are more contemporary. Mixing styles can be interesting, but it takes design confidence to do it well. For instance, classic toile de Jouy curtains can be combined with rustic rattan blinds in the right setting. Window dressings in a contrasting style can be used to tone down the negative aspects of a room's design. Instead of frilly curtains, a cellular shade may keep an English country room looking fresh. Similarly, velvet drapery can add warmth to a contemporary living room, where vertical blinds may be too stark. To develop a trained eye for creating unusual combinations, look at interiors in magazines and visit designer showhouses.

Most arrangements can be successfully designed by complementing the existing decor rather than mixing styles. For a romantic bedroom, nothing beats billowing sheers or the soft

Opposite: Full-length draperies and a matching swag valance add the crowning touch to this formal dining room. The heavy, lined silk fabric and the finishing details coordinate well with the room's traditional furnishings.

Left: In this dual-function room, which serves as a study or as a dining area as needed, bamboo shades reinforce the overall look of relaxed elegance.

silhouette of a balloon shade. The crisp lines of miniblinds enhance the simplicity of a modern living room. Gingham café curtains bring to mind country-style kitchens.

Also consider the decorating and architectural style of your home when planning your arrangement. How will the curtains or shades that you choose fit into the grand scheme? Visualize how the house will look from room to room,

indoors and out. Although the window dressings in different rooms don't have to match, they should coordinate—particularly if you can see one space from another. Picture a hall that leads into a living room. The swags in the hall can be light green, picking up an accent color from the living-room curtain's floral print, for example. In this case, each space has its own style of treatment, but they are unified by a coordinating color.

THREE Turn the window into a focal point, or make it blend with the decor. A window that takes center stage in the room's design should be dramatic. Strong patterns or vibrant colors are both ways to grab attention, especially if the treatment itself is fairly plain. Elaborate layers of drapery with toppers, such as swags, valances, and cornices, steal the spotlight, too. Embellishments can do the trick—think trimmings, tassels, and rosettes. A word of caution, however: when making a focal point out of an arrangement, don't let it overpower the room.

Windows that blend into a room's design create a serene ambiance. To create a low-key background, choose fabrics or colors that exactly match the walls. Neutral hues and pastels are equally soothing. Sheers add a softness and delicacy that is never intrusive.

COLOR

You can use warm colors and cool colors effectively to manipulate the way that a window treatment is perceived. Because warm colors appear to advance, windows swathed in sunny hues seem closer together, making a room feel intimate. Conversely, cool tones and neutrals appear to recede and can be used to open up a smaller space. However, these color tricks can be employed more subtly. The less-intense version of a color will generally reduce its apparent tendency to advance or recede. Generally speaking, two contrasting colors, such as blue and orange, have the same impact as one dark color, reducing perceived space. Monochromatic schemes, on the other hand, visually enlarge space, while neutrals of similar value make window treatments retreat. Keep these effects in mind when choosing a fabric color.

SMARTtip   Mixing Patterns

A trick for mixing patterns is to provide links of scale, motif, and color. The regularity of checks, stripes, textural looks, and geometrics, particularly if small-scale and low-contrast, tends to make them easy-to-mix "neutral" patterns. A small floral can play off a thin ticking stripe, while a cabbage-rose chintz may require a bolder stripe as a same-scale foil. Use the same or similar patterns in varying sizes, or develop a theme by focusing on florals, geometric, or ethnic prints.

Opposite: Dramatic color makes this window the undeniable focal point here. The curtain fabric also introduces yet another pattern into a busy, but confident, decor.

Left: Blue and yellow is a popular color combination. Here, both of these hues share a similar value, which keeps the impact of so many patterns subtle and pretty.

Below: The window treatments in this living room are intentionally understated. The designer accomplished this by relying on a subtle pattern.

PATTERN

Fabric is one of the most popular ways to add pattern to a room. Because pattern is largely a vehicle for color, the same rules that guide the selection of color effectively narrow the field when it comes to selecting a pattern or complement of patterns. The designer's old friend, scale, from Chapter 2, page 22, is the other important consideration when picking and mixing patterns.

A large-scale pattern is like a warm color in that it appears to come toward you. It can create a lively and stimulating atmosphere and generally make a large space seem cozier. In a small space, handle a large-scale pattern with care, or it can overpower the room. That doesn't mean rule it out completely, but perhaps use it sparingly. A small-scale pattern appears to recede, making a small space seem larger. In a large room, the effect of a small pattern can be bland. From a distance it may read as a single color. If you're using a small-scale pattern on window treatments in a large space, pick one with vibrant colors.

TEXTURE

Window treatments are a natural outlet for texture. Fabric choices for draperies and curtains, as well as the fabrics and other materials available for blinds and shades, are enormous and varied. Texture can be enhanced by the way fabric is hung. Pleating, for example, creates a play of light and shadow that looks three-dimensional. You can combine layers of fabric and blinds to show off different textures.

Texture doesn't have the obvious impact on a window treatment that color and pattern wield. Its influence is subtle. But whether a material is soft or hard, smooth or rough, glossy or matte, the texture will suggest something about the overall look that color or pattern alone cannot. A variety of textures plays upon the senses and adds a layer of complexity and sophistication to a design. As with every aspect of decorating, mixing textures involves a balancing act. To give a room a distinct character, you might let one texture predominate, but the right contrast can be intriguing.

FABRICS AND TEXTURES

One of the easiest ways to introduce texture into a design is with fabric. Brocades and damasks, moirés and chenilles, tweeds and chintzes—all conjure up different looks and sen-

Opposite: An over-scale pattern on the windows modifies the proportions and perception of this space. A room that could feel large and impersonal instead looks lively.

Right: A tiny office under the attic eaves appears cheerful and airy thanks to a lightweight curtain fabricated from a smooth, almost sheer cotton voile.

sations. Coarse and matte fabrics, such as tweed, wool, tapestry, and velvet, absorb light and sound. Glossy and smooth fabrics, which range from silk and satin to chintz and taffeta, reflect light.

Before selecting a fabric, you should know that texture can affect your perception of a particular space. For example, coarse or matte fabrics on the window will make a room seem smaller and cozier than it actually is. You can use this attribute to your decorating advantage. If you have a room that is too big, too expansive, or too impersonal (such as a family room with a vaulted ceiling), tapestry draperies or wool panels will make the space feel snug. Smooth and shiny fabrics do the reverse: they make a room look larger and brighter. Small or dark areas will benefit from pale-colored silk curtains. Light reflected off the fabric will make the room look open or less stuffy.

A fabric's weave affects color, so test a sample of the material in the room. Think of how the gray color of a tweed jacket looks "heathered" and muted. On a silk shirt, however, the same gray color is shimmery and more intense—a completely different effect. Texture can also either soften or enhance a pattern. Patterns are crisp on glazed chintz but are blurred on chennille. A coarsely textured surface tones down the intensity of a color and gives the color subtle variations.

PULLING IT ALL TOGETHER

You've analyzed your room's decor, and you've established whether you want the window treatment to be a focal point. Now you need to choose a color scheme, as well as mix and match fabric patterns. How do you find the best shade and pick the right pattern?

One way designers analyze the colors, patterns, and textures for a window treatment is to put together a sample board. The white, foam-cored presentation board sold in art-supply stores, measuring at least 8½ x 11 inches, is ideal for this purpose. Attach to the board with rubber cement (or tack to it with removable sticky material) any swatches of fabric, linings, and trimmings that you're considering. (If you are decorating the entire room as well as choosing treatments, it is a good idea to include paint color chips, wallpaper samples, and fabric swatches for the furnishings so that everything can be compared together.) Keep swatches and other items in the same proportion on the board as they would be on the window. For example, a fabric sample that you're considering for the curtain panels will be large, whereas the lining in an accent color for a swag will take up far less space. Add and remove things as you experiment with different looks, and be certain to look at the board in the room for which it's created at different times of the day under both natural and artificial light.

a gallery of smart ideas

1 In a country dining room, a casual unstructured swag strikes the right note of informality.

2 These curtains can be tied back during the day and closed at night.

3 A layered look adds interest to these simple windows.

4 Natural-fiber shades enhance the indoor-outdoor feeling of this bath.

5 A large-pattern print sets the style in this room.

6 A blue paisley scarf over a lace shade lends a French accent to this kitchen.

DOLLARS AND SENSE

LIFESTYLE ■ ASSESSING YOUR BUDGET ■ HIRING A PROFESSIONAL

Decorating decisions of all kinds, including those related to selecting window treatments, should be made sensibly and in accordance with lifestyle and budget. For example, costly goblet-pleat drapery made of white slubbed silk may be an elegant choice in a living room, but not if the children play there. Heavy or tied treatments that need daily opening and closing are not smart choices, either, if older, stiffer hands and fingers have to make the adjustments.

When it comes to planning the budget, realistically look at how much you have to spend and how much you *should* spend. Curtains for a rented apartment or a seasonal house generally call for less of an investment than drapery for a long-term or year-round family home. How much you want to spend also determines whether to order custom window treatments, buy ready-made versions, or make them yourself. The first option typically includes professional installation and cleaning. Complex designs often require special skills because the window treatments are actually constructed on the window itself. Ready-made window treatments are offered in a variety of sizes to fit standard windows. Some, but not all, are washable. The style of home-sewn curtains depends on your level of skill. (For making basic curtains, see how-to directions in Chapter 12, "Create It Yourself.")

LIFESTYLE

In the previous chapter, you analyzed the room's function, noting any special needs or unusual problems that you have to address. Now you must examine your family's lifestyle. How you live influences all of your decorating decisions, and window treatments are no exception. What follows is a list of questions to help you identify these lifestyle issues. As you review these questions, don't just make mental notes of the answers. Write them down. That way, you can refer to your responses on a regular basis. This will help you stay on track all through the process.

■ **Personal Preference.** What type of interior do you prefer? Window treatments can enhance—or even change—the overall atmosphere of a room. For example, after a long day at the office, you may want to relax in a soothing interior. Soft colors set the mood. Add curtains with a blackout lining, and you can darken a bedroom at will. Do you need a more stimulating space? Fabrics in cheerful colors or sheers that let in filtered light may do the trick. Do you like the look of a window dressed in several layers, such as a swag-and-jabot valance over drapery and undercurtains? Or do you prefer just one or two elements to achieve the desired effect?

■ **Location.** Start by asking yourself how long you will be staying in this space. Is it a permanent family home? Are you renting? Do you have a long-term or a short-term lease?

Is this a second home, used only during specific seasons? Seasonal spaces have their own special considerations.

Window treatments may need to be dirt-resistant because the house will be shut up for part of the year. They may also need to be particularly durable if many different people will be renting the house.

Where you live can be as important a consideration as how you live. For a home in the city, privacy may be a greater issue than for a home in a suburban or rural area. Even where privacy is not a factor, relatively bare windows may make some family members uncomfortable. At night, the blackness of an uncovered window can have a chilling effect, particularly for those who grew up in homes where the curtains were always drawn snug at night.

■ **External Appearances.** Does your house have a particular architectural style that is more compatible with certain types of window treatments? Because you must consider how a treatment looks from the outside of the home, this factor should play a part in your decision. For example, vertical blinds may not be appropriate for a traditional-style or historic house, yet may pair seamlessly with a house that has modern architecture. Exterior symmetry also may be important, particularly on the windows at the front of the house. What does this mean? Consider the curbside view. Treating the front windows in dramatically different styles may not have a pleasing effect on the overall exterior appearance of your house.

Opposite: These custom-designed shoji screens easily slide on a track to cover or reveal the windows. They also reinforce the Asian simplicity of the room.

Above: A simple valance can be an affordable way to soften the look of practical shades or blinds while adding color and pattern to a window.

Right: Standard-size Roman shades are easy to install yourself. Here, they unobtrusively serve a pair of windows and a breathtaking view.

SMARTtip   Protocol

It's generally a good idea to delay any final decisions about window treatments until you have determined your wall finishes, floor coverings, and overall color scheme. This way, your room's personality will be fully developed and the treatment you choose will complement the entire room. Rods, finials, and the like can be viewed as accessories, rather than hardware, that reflect the essence of the room. In addition, if you are considering a simple treatment or relatively uncovered windows, this will give you the luxury of time to decide whether you are comfortable with the look.

■ **Family Members.** The number of people in a household is another point to consider. Are you single? Newlyweds? A retired couple? A family? If you have a family, how old are the children? Are there other dependents in the house, such as an elderly parent?

Single people and couples tend to have more choices and fewer restrictions. They don't have to take into account the tastes and habits of others in the household. Plus, there is less wear and tear on all of the furnishings, including window treatments. However, if young children are frequent visitors, toddler-friendly window treatments—ones without dangling cords and puddled draperies—may be in order.

Families with young children should be realistic about their choices. Custom-made drapery in an expensive fabric, such as silk, may be too delicate or too costly to repeatedly have cleaned after repeated assaults by grimy little hands. Attractive, washable cotton curtains, shutters with a pretty valance, or swags with short or sill-length jabots may be more practical. Also, remember that the rules for behavior

Left: Fabric shades in a city apartment will have to hold up to the grime and airborne pollutants that abound in urban environments.

Opposite: Curtains in a little girl's room feature a fabric that isn't too juvenile and will "grow up" with her.

that apply in your home may not be the same in the homes of your children's friends. Playing hide-and-go-seek behind the curtains can happen as quickly as your back is turned. It's simply easier to avoid potential hassles.

If you are caring for someone who is elderly or who has a disability, think about the weight of the window treatment you may be installing and its ease of operation before you make a final selection. Adaptations are available to make some window treatments less difficult to handle. For example, push-button mechanisms can be installed to raise and lower Roman shades or to draw heavy drapery closed. Blinds with continuous-loop cords are easier to adjust than those with pull cords.

Pets can influence your choice of treatment, too. If your dog likes to curl up in cozy places, puddled curtains that billow onto the floor are not a good idea. If your cat is indiscriminate about where he sharpens his claws, choose a style that will be out of his reach, such as shutters or sill-length curtains. And even well-behaved pets may shed. A black Labrador retriever brushing past floor-length light-colored curtains can only mean more frequent vacuuming. Shorter curtains or pet-coordinated colors may lighten your housekeeping chores.

■ **Maintenance.** Don't overlook maintenance. If a treatment requires frequent or expensive cleaning, consider whether it is right for you. For instance, if you travel often, you may not have the time to maintain formal drapery. The same is true if you have a house full of children—you don't need another task added to your list. Low-maintenance window treatments, such as blinds that can be easily dusted and a washable valance, may require less time and expense. This is not to say that formal treatments can't be low-maintenance—a simple a pair of stationary panels may only need regular vacuuming to keep their good looks. But a multilayered window confection of double swags with cascade tails, rosettes, trimmed curtains, and sheers will take more attention. When heavy cleaning becomes necessary, you will probably have to call in a professional to dismantle the window covering, dry clean it, and re-hang it. If your budget and lifestyle allow for these

things, however, such designs have unparalleled decorative impact and they may be worth the expense of the special upkeep.

Now take a look at any existing window treatments. What's in place now may be a cue to the style and function of the new drapery. Assess both the good and bad points of the existing treatments. What do you like about them? Are there any problems? What should the new treatments do that these don't?

ASSESSING YOUR BUDGET

Figuring out a budget involves more than just finding out the price of a window treatment that you like. You must weigh the cost against the amount of money you have to spend, and how much it will take to maintain it. You also have to factor in how long you expect the treatment to last. In a rental apartment, you might want something that choose is flexible enough to take with you when you leave. If you've just bought your own home, and intend to renovate in a few years, take those plans into account. If you're retired, and this is your ultimate dream house, you maywant to pull out all of the stops and go for something that you've always wanted.

Opposite: Easy-care looks can be as fashionable as more elaborate designs while requiring much less effort. Here, the shades are part of an ensemble cast of understated but tasteful furnishings.

Left: A full formal treatment will grab a lot of attention in a room, especially if the proportions are grand and the materials are elegant and upscale. Here, gorgeous fabric and trims make a sweeping statement around French doors.

and find out about the fees for its services as well as the cost of installation. Because you haven't made any final decisions about the style, keep in mind that the prices you are gathering are only rough estimates. The purpose is to educate yourself about the cost of the various components so that you will be able to make realistic choices that are within your budget. If the costs seem too high, you might want to begin to explore some alternative routes, such as watching for sales or shopping the discount stores. If you are handy with a sewing machine, research some styles that are easy to make. Check out the pattern catalogs for some useful ideas. If you are considering the make-it-yourself alternative, be realistic about your capabilities. And remember to factor in your time as part of the cost.

TWO Choose a style Now that you are familiar with pricing, you can hone in on the window treatment that suits your style and pocketbook. Review all of the stylistic possibilities. For a thorough guide to the choices, use Chapters 5, 6, and 7, which completely cover draperies and curtains; shades, blinds, and shutters; and cornices, valances, and swags. Now is also the time to decide what *type* of window treatment you plan to install: custom (through an interior designer), ready-made or semi-custom (through a retailer), or home sewn. If you don't want to go the custom-made route but are unsure about the style and color, look for an interior designer who will work with you on a consultant basis. For an hourly fee, he or she can help you narrow down the styles, fabrics, and colors that will best suit your needs and your decor.

How a room is used may also influence your budget decisions. For example, if you entertain frequently, particularly for business purposes, then you may want to allocate a larger part of your budget to window treatments in the "public" rooms. If you are planning curtains for a baby's room, remember that what is cute for an infant's nursery may be all wrong for the room of a school-age child.

SMART steps | **ONE** Become familiar with the costs of materials and services. Start by visiting showrooms, custom window-treatment shops, and home centers. Also call for catalogs with ready-made examples. Compare the prices. Evaluate everything, including the fabric, the lining, and the interlining, so you are comparing apples to apples. Don't forget the details: take a look at hardware, such as holdbacks, poles, and finials, as well as tiebacks, tassels, and trimmings. If you are considering a custom treatment, talk to a design firm

THREE Calculate the costs. Add up the price of the materials (face fabric, lining, and interlining, if any), trimmings, hardware, rods, and labor. As a safety net, add 15 to

Planning a Window Treatment in Stages

Stage One

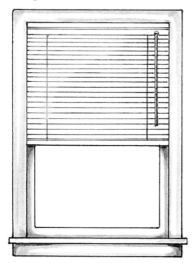

If you're on a budget, decorate your window in stages. Stage One is a covering for privacy, such as blinds. Stage Two can be a layer of drapery panels and a traverse rod. Stage Three adds details, such as a shaped cornice and silk tiebacks with tassels.

Stage Two

Stage Three

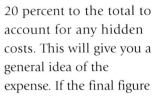

Opposite: A large bay of French doors or windows is a natural location for a grand gesture. Selecting the right fabric and design that will complement all of the decorative elements in the room requires skill and, often, a trained eye.

Right: The more poufs, the prettier the balloon shade, and so you mustn't skimp on fabric. Get professional assistance when taking measurements for a curtain or shade that will be tailored to fit.

20 percent to the total to account for any hidden costs. This will give you a general idea of the expense. If the final figure is beyond your means, you have two options. First, because this is the planning stage, you can still easily make some money-saving changes. Choose a less-expensive fabric, such as a cotton instead of linen, or simplify the design: switch from labor-intensive goblet pleats to a gathered heading or opt not to use an interlining. However, you may not want to compromise on the design. If so, try the second approach, which involves doing the window treatments in stages. For example, a multilayered design may have a miniblinds, lined drapery, silk rope tiebacks with tassels, and a shaped cornice. Start by installing the most necessary element of the design—in this case, the miniblinds for light and privacy control. When you have the money, you can add the next layer, which consists of the drapery and the traverse rod. The last elements to be put into place are the luxurious extras—the cornice and the tasseled tiebacks.

HIRING A PROFESSIONAL

If you want professional help, do some homework. Ask your friends and neighbors for referrals. Visit show houses; participate in house tours. These events, usually held to benefit local charities, offer you a chance to see the work of regional design talent. Check out the home-fashion articles in local magazines and newspapers. Sometimes retail establishments can recommend professionals. Search the Internet for design organizations that can make recommendations. Then, make an appointment with several professionals. They may visit your home, or you may ask to visit their workroom. Look at their portfolios. Ask for at least three references—and call and check them. It's also a good idea to contact the Better Business Bureau to make sure that there are no complaints against the professional you plan to hire.

a gallery of smart ideas

1 Decorator details add personality to this semi-custom design.

2 A coordinated look can be effort-lessly achieved by using the same fabric for each layer of a window treatment.

3 Great style can come from retail as well as decora-tor sources.

4 An interior designer can suggest a unique look for a wall of modern windows.

5 Roman shades come in standard as well as custom sizes today.

6 Tassel trimming elevates this simple swag into a rich-looking treatment.

7 An understated design always looks chic, what-ever the cost.

3

4

5

6

7

CURTAINS AND DRAPERIES

CURTAIN BASICS ▪ WHAT'S YOUR STYLE? ▪
ROD-POCKET AND GATHERED HEADINGS ▪
PLEATED HEADINGS ▪
TABBED AND TIED HEADINGS ▪
PIERCED AND PLAIN HEADINGS

Long ago, but not so far in the past, curtains were just a way to keep out the cold or extreme light. Today, these fabric-based coverings can still be used to control the amount of natural light in a room and limit heat gain in the summer and heat loss during the winter. But technology and the modern insulating qualities of glass allow curtains and draperies to be more, or even less, than practical. With limitless combinations of fabric, color, and trim, these window treatments can be simply decorative.

Throughout this book, the terms "draperies" and "curtains" are used interchangeably. But to some people, they have slightly different meanings. *Draperies* are usually pleated, lined, and floor length, with a tailored, formal style. They are attached via hooks to a traverse rod; a cord mechanism is used to close them. *Curtains* are normally suspended from rods by rings, tabs, ties, or a rod-pocket casing; they look less formal.

When choosing curtains or draperies for your windows, make note of how far you will be able to retract the panels. *Stack-back* refers to how compactly curtains or draperies can be drawn back on a rod. When there is minimal wall space around a window or when you want to maximize a view, the depth of the stack-back is a concern.

CURTAIN BASICS

Curtains encompass three basic styles: panels, cafés, and tiers. Heading variations, including pocket casings, tabs, loops, ties, grommets, and pleats, can change the personality of each style. In addition, curtains can be lined, unlined, or—for extra body and insulation—interlined. All of these elements work together to influence the ultimate appearance of your window treatment.

TYPES OF CURTAINS

The basic *panel* is the most versatile and straightforward type of window dressing. It can be any length and have any type of heading. It can be hung straight, without any adornment, or tied back in one of the various positions. It looks wonderful with all sorts of hardware, including traverse rods, decorative poles with finials, curtain rings, café clips, tiebacks, and holdbacks. This multipurpose treatment can be made in a variety of fabrics with trimmings—from fringe to gimp—to reflect any decor.

A *café curtain* covers the lower half of a window. A longer version goes approximately three-quarters up the window, leaving a small section at the top of the window exposed. Café curtains are usually hung from a pole by rings, clips, tabs, ties, or a rod-pocket heading. This type of casual treatment suits cottage-style interiors. Similar to café curtains, *tiered curtains* are a team of two half curtains covering the upper and lower sections of a window. They, too, have a homey, comfortable ambiance and are hung on curtain rods.

CURTAIN LENGTHS

The curtain length influences the style of the treatment. A sill-length curtain has a casual air; drapery that falls to the floor connotes elegance. Curtain lengths also affect activity in the area near a window. Are the windows close to a breakfast table? If so, shorter curtains are less intrusive and leave clearance around the table. Is there a heat source underneath the window? Curtains should never touch or block a radiator, heat vent, or heating unit. Is the treatment hung on or around a glazed door? Make sure that it doesn't block the opening and that you can open and close the door—and the curtain, if desired—easily.

Curtain lengths can camouflage problems, too. Is the window awkwardly shaped? Or is there an architectural flaw that you would like to conceal? A floor-length treatment, hung above the window frame, can help disguise the problem. In some rooms, windows may be different widths and lengths. If this is the case, plan the largest window treatment first. Dress the remaining windows in a scaled-down version of this treatment. For visual unity, install all the upper hardware at the same height.

In general, a window treatment looks best when it falls in line with the sill or floor. The most common lengths for drapery are sill, below sill, floor, and puddled. As the description implies, a *sill-length* curtain skims the windowsill. Favored for horizontal windows, it can start from the top of the window to the sill or, when café style, from the middle of the window to the sill. A curtain at this length is typically easy to operate, so it is a good choice for a window that will be opened and closed often.

The *below-sill length* falls at least 4 inches beneath the window frame so that it covers the apron, the horizontal board that runs under the sill. If the curtain is too far below the sill, however, it looks awkward and unfinished. A sill-length panel, too, can be used for café or three-quarter curtains, and it can cover up an unattractive window frame. It generally looks best on picture windows and above window seats.

A *floor-length curtain* makes a strong visual statement. Make sure that the curtain is only ½ inch above the floor

Opposite: These floor-length curtain panels feature a pleated heading. Small curtain, or drapery, hooks are used to attach the panels to the rings that run across the rod.

Below: The hems of these kitchen curtains sit slightly above the sills of the two windows. When same-size windows are adjacent, the curtains should be exactly the same length.

Too Short

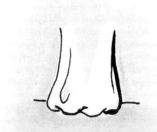

Too Long

Correct

because, like a hem that's too high on pants, floor-length treatments that fall short can suffer the "floods." (In humid areas, however, the curtain can be an inch off the floor to allow for the rise and fall of the fabric.) If you install layered drapery, the inner curtain can be ¼ to ½ inch shorter than the outer curtain. To avoid seeing the back of the heading from the outside, add 4 inches to the curtain's length so that it hangs above the window frame. This length works well with double-hung windows, bay windows, sliding glass doors, and tall, narrow openings, such as French doors.

Puddling is the term used for a floor-length curtain with an extra allowance of fabric that is arranged into a soft pouf (the puddle) on the floor. This is a dramatic length that falls 6 to 8 inches onto the floor. (For the correct length, see the

SMARTtip   Curtain Weights

A breeze can stir up a floor-length curtain, leaving it in disarray. A curtain weight can minimize the problem, plus it helps drapery to hang more smoothly. You will find two types of curtain weights: disk weights and fabric-covered weights. A disk weight is a small, round piece of lead that is inserted into the hem at each corner and each seam. To prevent it from rubbing and wearing out the fabric, insert it into a pocket made of lining fabric or muslin. A fabric-covered weight consists of links of metal encased in a fabric tube. This type, which comes in different sizes to correspond to the weight of the fabric, is attached along the hem.

Opposite: In an older home, windows may be out of plumb, which could make long panels appear to be different lengths. To camouflage this, puddle the hemlines on the floor.

Below: Ventilation is important in a bathroom, and so curtains should not interfere with the operation of a window. These sill-length panels are unobtrusive.

illustrations on the opposite page.) Particularly appropriate for floor-to-ceiling windows, puddling has some drawbacks. A puddled curtain often needs adjustment, as it can be easily disarranged. Also, it isn't the right choice for high-traffic aisles or doorways, because the extra fabric can block the function of a door or cause someone to trip.

High Tie

Midway Ties

Center Tie

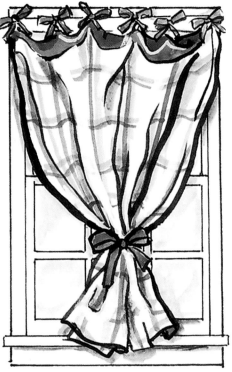

TIEBACK POSITIONS

How a curtain frames an opening is an important part of a window dressing's overall design. You can leave a curtain hanging unadorned, but by using a tieback, you can create a sculpted silhouette of fabric against a window. You can also control the amount of light that comes into the room and create a dramatic frame that enhances a view or covers an unsightly one.

Where you position the tieback affects the way a curtain hangs. The curtain can be caught back in a dramatic swoop of fabric, or it can be gently held open, revealing a colorful contrasting lining. The traditional tieback positions—high, midway, and low—are some of the most effective placements. Looping a tieback around or just below a pole, angled *high*, creates a short curve of fabric; don't use this arrangement where the curtain is moved often. A tieback positioned *midway* shouldn't fall exactly in the center; the best placement is slightly above or below the middle of the cur-

tain. Two-thirds of the way down the curtain is the proper place for a *low* tieback. When using this position, check that a tasseled tieback doesn't brush the floor, however.

A *center tie*—when one or two curtains are gathered at the middle so that they curve on both sides—can look impressive if it's on a bay or bow window. Use a rope tieback or, if the material is lightweight, literally knot the fabric. A *crisscross* arrangement requires two curtain rods and looks best with lightweight or sheer fabrics. When each panel is caught midway, the top halves overlap.

To create a *bishop's sleeve*, arrange two center ties at different points on a curtain (one high, one midway). Pull out the fabric above each tie to create a double tier of soft poufs. Try an *angled double tie* with a sheer undertreatment because the sinuous outline stands out against a gauzy backdrop. Slightly different from the bishop's sleeve, the two ties are arranged at the high and midway points on the panel so that the curtain swoops into graceful curves on only one side of the window.

Low Ties

Crisscrossed Ties

Angled Double Ties

SMART tip

To make the folds fall evenly, train the curtains by tying them back for 48 hours or more. This is a process known as dressing the curtain and results in drapery that holds its shape and hangs well. To start, draw the drapery into the stack-back position. Fix the pleats and gaps in the heading until you are pleased with the arrangement. If the treatment is hanging below a curtain rod, position the gaps to fold toward the back; if the curtain hangs in front of the rod or pole, the gaps will fold forward. Smooth each pleat from the heading downward as far as possible. Then work from the bottom upward, gathering the pleats together. With a strip of fabric, make a loose tie just below the heading to hold the pleats in place. Tie another fab-

How to Dress a Curtain

ric strip midway down the curtain, smoothing the pleats as you go. Follow with a tie near the hemline. The ties should be tight enough to hold the fabric without marking it. Next, steam the curtains with a hand steamer. You may need a friend to hold the curtain while you fasten the ties. Leave the curtains undisturbed for a couple of days before removing the ties.

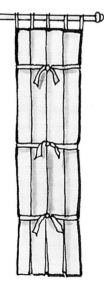

Left: Full formal draperies are installed just under the crown molding in this dining room. The symmetrical tails on the swag valance feature rosettes on the corners.

Opposite: The floor-length curtains in this study have a blackout lining that completely blocks out the sun when the panels are drawn shut.

WHAT'S YOUR STYLE?

Whether you are choosing curtains for an entire house or just one room, the process is the same. You need to make three basic decisions about your treatment. Will it be formal or informal? Lined or unlined? What type of heading? Once these decisions are made, you can finalize a design.

FORMAL VERSUS INFORMAL STYLE

A room's window treatments are influenced by a number of elements, including the function of the space, the architectural style of the house, and the decorating preferences of the homeowner. The result is that the same windows can be treated quite differently. For example, picture a dining room with a bay window. That type of window is often given a multilayered, floor-length window dressing—in other words, a formal window treatment. But if you prefer a more casual style, you can choose the informal look of café curtains with sill-length, tied-back side panels.

A Full Formal Treatment. Formal treatments often involve two or three layers. One layer, called the *casement curtain*, is installed inside the window's trim area. Typically it's a sheer, solid, or lace panel that lays straight or is gathered at the top. *Overdraperies*, often referred to simply as draperies, make up the second layer. Generally, they cover the window and the trim and, space permitting, extend beyond to the sides or the area above the window. The third, and optional, layer of a full formal window treatment is a *valance*, sometimes called a pelmet, which runs horizontally across the top of the window and covers the drapery or curtain heading. A hard valance, also called a *cornice* or a *lambrequin*, is usually made of wood and covered with fabric or upholstery. To some eyes, the window treatment is unfinished without this last element, but this is strictly a matter of taste. (See Chapter 7, "Top Treatments," page 100.) Luxurious, heavyweight fabrics, such as damasks, brocades, silks, tapestries, and velvets, enhance the sophistication of formal treatments. However, remember that these fabrics require professional cleaning every couple of years.

An Informal Treatment. Informal treatments may consist of one or two layers or nothing at all. If location and privacy considerations permit, a beautiful window looks attractive without a dressing—especially when there's also something pleasant to see outside. Sometimes simple casement curtains look attractive in casual rooms. If only the lower half of the window needs covering, café curtains offer privacy without blocking light. Fabrics that lend themselves to an informal look include all cottons, such as chintz, ticking, toile de Jouy, linen, gingham, and muslin. Unlike the fabric that is typical of formal draperies, most of these are washable.

LINING

The style of curtains—formal or informal—often dictates whether the treatment will be lined. Other considerations include how much natural light you want in a room and how long you expect the arrangement to last.

Unlined Curtains. An *unlined* curtain diffuses daylight, but it does not exclude it. It is the simplest form of window dressing, and it is effective on its own or as an undertreatment. Because an unlined treatment lacks the extra thickness of a lining, it stacks back tightly. Choose a fabric with

no right or wrong side so that it looks equally attractive from both the outside and inside of the window. Voile, lace, muslin, and sheers made of cotton or silk organza are the classic fabric choices for unlined treatments. Textured fabrics with open weaves are also suitable.

An unlined curtain filters light beautifully and provides a hazy screen from prying eyes. However, because it offers little privacy in the evening when lamps are turned on, consider pairing sheers with shades or blinds. (See Chapter 6, "Shades, Blinds, and Shutters," on page 78.) Sunlight damage is another drawback to unlined curtains. Without a protective lining, the fabric deteriorates quickly.

Lined Curtains. A *lined* curtain has body, improving its appearance by creating softer, deeper folds. A lining blocks sunlight, protecting the curtain fabric and other elements in

the room from fading, particularly where there is western or southern exposure. Sunlight also adds a yellow tint to unlined fabric that may throw off your room's color scheme. A lining preserves the true color of the face fabric. Linings increase privacy, reduce outside noise, and block drafts and dust. Check for linings treated to resist rot and sun damage. Once a lining has deteriorated, the curtain can be relined or hung without the lining. To achieve the best protection possible, buy the best quality lining fabric that you can afford.

If you line one curtain in a room, do the same to the rest so that the color and drape of the curtains match. Typically, lining fabric comes in white or off-white. Although colored linings are available, be aware that light shining through a lining affects the hue of a lightweight curtain fabric. Get samples of your intended lining and curtain fabric, and then test them together at the window for color change.

Interlinings. If you are set on having a colored lining, consider adding an *interlining*, which is a soft, blanket-like layer of material that is sandwiched between the lining and the curtain fabric. Like a lining, it increases the insulation and light-blocking qualities of the drapery, as well as extending the life of the curtains. It also gives a professional fin-

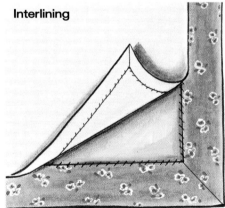

Interlining

Left: Lots of unlined gathered cotton fabric keeps this bedroom light while providing a sense of soft enclosure.

Opposite: A floral contrast lining with a transition border is disarming when the panels are pulled back.

ish to pleats by improving the drape of the fabric. A lining is usually sewn on, but it can also be attached with special double tape or pinned on with buttonholes that slip over drapery hooks. The latter allows the lining and face fabric to be cleaned separately. If you need a dark bedroom during the daytime because you work nights, try a *blackout lining*, which almost completely blocks sunlight. Other specialty linings include insulating and reflective types. These types of linings can be sewn on, but they can also be hung on a separate rod and drawn closed only when needed.

CURTAIN HEADINGS

The *heading* is the top of the curtain. Headings encompass a variety of styles—from a simple casing, or fabric pocket, to complex folds that are intricately pleated. Some headings, such as tied or tabbed styles, tend to be casual, while others, such as goblet and cartridge pleats, are formal.

Rod-Pocket and Gathered Headings

Gathered Heading

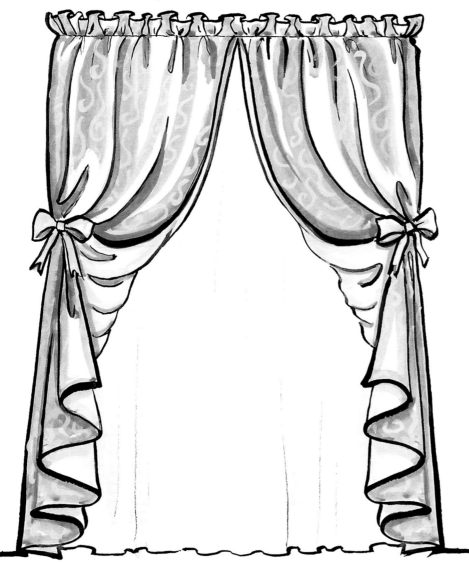

A simple design is often the most effective one, which is true of rod-pocket and gathered headings. A rod-pocket heading, also known as a slot heading, is a casing (a tunnel-like pocket) created by turning the top of the curtain fabric down twice and then stitching it along the bottom fold. The rod is then slipped into the casing, and the curtain is gathered.

A rod-pocket heading can be plain, which means it lays flush against the rod, or it can have a ruffle. This ruffle is typically 2 to 4 inches deep.

Because it is difficult to reposition the fabric on the rod, choose a rod-pocket heading in situations where the curtain remains stationary. This unpretentious heading pairs well with a short, lightweight style. However, a curtain with a rod-pocket heading can also be lined and extended to the floor.

Rod Sleeve. When a rod-pocket heading is used on large openings, such as a picture window or a sliding glass door, the curtains purposely remain at the sides of the opening, leaving the rod exposed. If you don't like this look, try unifying the treatment with a rod sleeve. Used in place of a valance, a rod sleeve is

Rod-Pocket Heading

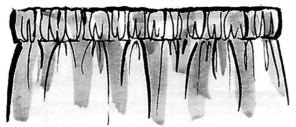

Ruffled Rod-Pocket Heading

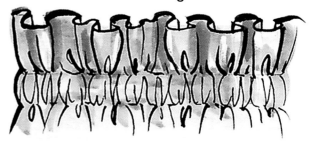

a simple casing that is gathered over the rod to visually bridge the gap between the curtain panels. Match the style and fabric of the sleeve to the heading. If the heading has a ruffle, try a sleeve with a double ruffle—one above and one below the casing—to add detail.

GATHERED HEADINGS

A gathered heading is a soft, 2- to 4-inch ruffle created by draw-cord tape, a strip of material with strings that are pulled to create the gathers. It hangs from curtain rings or hooks. An oversized ruffle, one that is 6 inches or more, creates a cuff—a valance-like edging—on a gathered heading. (A cuff can also be a separate piece of fabric attached to the top of the curtain panel.)

Bunched Heading. A rod-pocket or a gathered heading with an oversized ruffle can be converted into a bunched heading. This is achieved by pulling the ruffle's layers apart so that it is puffed up. (To add extra body, insert a piece of interlining into the heading.) The ruffle of a bunched heading can also be secured with stitches to create a scrunched effect. The larger the ruffle, the more pronounced this effect will be.

A gathered heading is compatible with most styles of curtains—long or short, lined or unlined. Because it is hung from curtain rings or hooks, it is easier to adjust than a rod-pocket heading. When a gathered heading is hung from curtain rings, it exposes a section of curtain rod, so pair it with hardware that has pizzazz. However, when it is hung from hooks, the traverse rod usually won't be visible.

Above: Loosely gathered fabric creates a dainty ruffle accent above this curtain's rod pocket. The fullness of the ruffle depends on the width of the rod.

Pleated Headings

Pleats offer the greatest design impact of all the headings. These elegant arrangements have a practical purpose, too: they create supple yet disciplined folds of fabric down the curtain length.

Pleat Types. The styles for pleated headings range from the subtly sophisticated to the impressively grand. The most common is the triple pleat, also known as the French or pinched pleat, which is a trio of folds pinched (gathered and secured) together at evenly spaced intervals along the top of the curtain. Reducing the number of folds to two creates a butterfly pleat. A fan pleat is made of three or more gathered folds that rise slightly above the rod so that the fabric scallops between the fans.

A pencil pleat is the approximate width of its namesake. It is part of an uninterrupted row of pleats. Because of the simplicity of this classic heading, use pencil pleats for draperies that are meant to blend with your room's decor rather than stand out; pencil pleats often top draperies that are tucked under valances or cornices. (See Chapter 7, "Top Treatments," page 100.) By fastening pencil pleats into a latticework pattern, an elaborate smocked heading is created. A box pleat is folded so that two pleats meet, creating flat planes of fabric; although used more often for valances, box pleats can work well for draperies, particularly contemporary or tailored styles.

For a dramatic treatment, the fold of a goblet pleat is formed into a cup-like shape above a pinch. To emphasize the

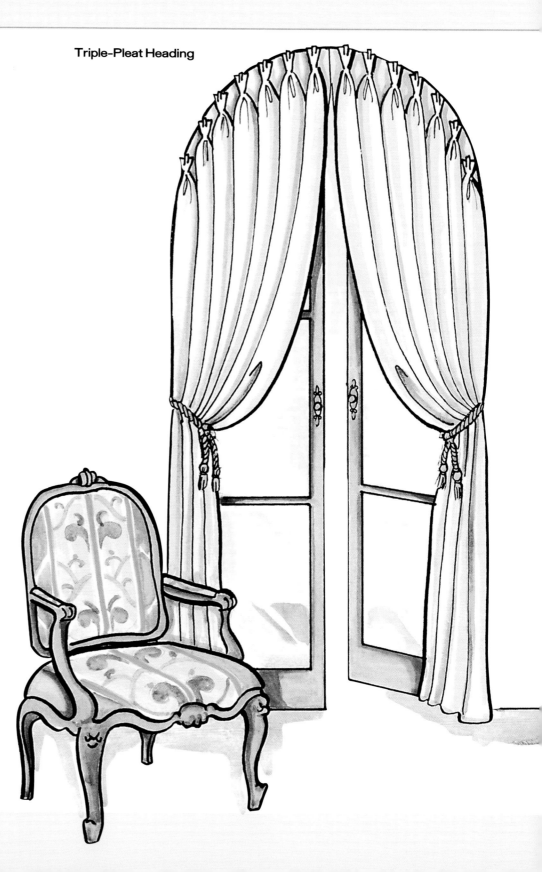

Triple-Pleat Heading

Fan-Pleat Heading

Pencil-Pleat Heading

Smocked Heading

Box-Pleat Heading

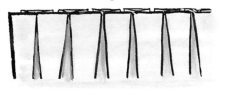

Goblet-Pleat Heading

Cartridge-Pleat Heading

shapes, cording is often attached by the pinch, linking each goblet in what is called a Flemish heading. A cartridge pleat is a tubular-shaped fold without a pinched section. Both goblet and cartridge pleats are usually stuffed with a small piece of lining or batting to pad the shapes; a piece of fabric in a contrasting color can be added on top of the stuffing to emphasize the shape of the design.

Stiffeners and Tapes. To look its best, a pleated heading requires a backing made of a stiffener, such as buckram—a course cloth stiffened with glue—or a tape to keep the design in a neat formation. If the pleats are hand-folded, buckram is used to make the heading firm. Buckram comes in 4- to 6-inch widths, and it is attached by sewing or, if the fusible type, ironing.

Pleating tape, which is a strip of cotton or nylon with strings running through it, gathers the curtain fabric into the desired type of pleats when the strings are pulled. The tape ranges from 1 to 5 inches wide and has pockets for inserting the drapery hooks. Like buckram, it can be sewn or fused to the back of the heading. Tapes provide good results if you are making pencil pleats, but complex headings, such as box, triple, and goblet pleats, turn out better made by hand with a buckram backing.

Pleated curtains are often lined and interlined to add fullness to them. Because of the extra weight from the lining and interlining, hang them securely from a stationary or a traverse rod; lightweight versions can hang from curtain rings on a curtain rod.

Right: Evenly spaced goblet pleats add a elegant straight line to the heading of this treatment. Curtain rings alllow the panels to glide easily across the pole.

Tabbed and Tied Headings

The casual elegance of tabbed and tied headings has recently grown in popularity. A tabbed heading is a looped piece of fabric with an exposed end (the tab) that is often adorned with a button; the button can be functional or decorative. Akin to a tabbed heading, a looped heading is a band of material without a visible tab end; it can be made of fabric, ribbon, or rope. Sometimes the fabric between the loops is scalloped, an effect favored for café curtains. A tied heading consists of two fabric strips that are tied in a bow onto a curtain rod.

Tabs, loops, and ties often look dressier when they are highlighted by fabric that contrasts with the curtain material. Another decorative accent for these headings is a cuff.

Even with a lining, these headings take up little stack-back space. However, tabbed and looped headings can be hard to adjust, so use both in stationary arrangements. By fastening a tied heading to curtain rings instead of directly onto the rod, it will move back and forth more smoothly.

Tabbed Heading

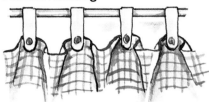

Tied Heading

Below: You can tie a bow or a knot in tabs such as these. Here they look less serious hanging casually from the pole.

Looped Heading

Pierced and Plain Headings

Because pierced and plain headings hang from grommets or rings, they are relatively easy to move. A pierced heading is a series of either buttonholes or grommets (eyelets) that perforate the top of a curtain. The curtain rod is threaded through these openings. To vary this heading, short pieces of ribbon or cord can be pulled through each grommet and tied to the rod. A curtain with a pierced heading can be lined. To help hold the shape, use a strip of buckram to reinforce and support the heading area.

Before making a pierced heading, always check that the curtain rod fits through the grommet. If you can't find a rod that is narrow enough, consider using curtain wire, which you can hang on brackets.

A plain heading, as the name implies, is simply hemmed without pleats or tape, and then attached to curtain rings or to café clips. A lining may be added, but the extra weight may be too much for café clips. Adorn a plain heading with cuffs, borders, or bows to add definition and form. Because the rod is visible, choose eye-catching hardware, especially a design that comes with handsome finials. You might consider a pole with a decorative painted finish.

Buckram makes a plain heading lay flat; for a softer look, try interfacing, a pliable material often used in dressmaking.

Right: A sheer lightweight fabric is ideal for a pierced heading. Here a good-looking iron rod adds style to the design.

Pierced Heading

Pierced Heading with Cord Tie

Plain Heading

a gallery of...

1 Cord makes an interesting tabbed heading.

2 Tiebacks accentuate goblet pleats.

3 Stripes play up the lines of drapery panels.

4 Lined, heavy curtains make a formal statement.

5 Lightweight cotton filters natural light.

6 Different styles, same fabric coordinate two rooms.

7 Sill-length curtains look great in a cozy cabin.

8 A folded-over length of fabric at the heading creates a stylish cuff.

...smart ideas

1 Appliqued leaves dress up simple curtain panels.

2 A ruffled valance adds a feminine touch to a lady's bedroom.

3 A contrasting edge draws attention to this curtain's heading as well as the architecture of the location.

4 A stiffener allows the attractive-curled effect of these ribbon tabs for an unusually pretty look.

5 Strong metal hold-backs that have been secured into the wall simply hold fabric. The design allows a window dressing that does not obscure a handsome window.

6 In a second-story bath, a café curtain provides privacy at the level where it is needed without overdressing the window.

7 Adjustable curtains on the lower half of the windows in this breakfast bay can be pushed back easily when the windows are opened for air.

5

6

7

CHAPTER 6

SHADES, BLINDS, AND SHUTTERS

PLEATED SHADES ▪ BASIC AND BATTEN SHADES ▪ FESTOON SHADES ▪ LOUVER BLINDS ▪ HORIZONTAL AND VERTICAL BLINDS ▪ LOUVER SHUTTERS ▪ SHOJI SCREENS

Shades, blinds, and shutters offer a variety of options for dressing the window and filtering the light. Some shades completely block the light when lowered, while others are designed to diffuse the sunlight that enters the room. And some shades can be raised to expose almost all of the window glass, while others can be only partially raised. Blinds, on the other hand, don't have to be raised to perform these same functions. Simply re-angling the slats does the trick. As a category, blinds impart a crisper, more tailored look to windows. Shutters, more than any other window treatment, bring an architectural element to the room. Other window treatments look like a fashion choice; shutters, once installed, appear to be an intrinsic part of the home's basic character, much like crown moldings and floorboards.

Any of these treatments can adorn a window as its single element, providing clean lines and a pared-down simplicity that goes with the modern aesthetic for interiors. But just as frequently, these treatments are one part of the total picture. Shades, blinds, and shutters can complement an existing window treatment in terms of fashion and supplement it in terms of function. Curtains, valances, cornices, swags and jabots, in all their many styles, add layers of decorating punch to these looks.

SHADES

A shade is a window treatment that is raised and lowered by means of a spring mechanism or cording system. This simple definition covers a great range of styles, from flat shades to softly draped festoon shades. Today, window-shade choices go far beyond the basic vinyl roller shade and into a whole world of exciting fashion choices. But before you decide which shade will grace your window, it is important to analyze your needs and understand your options.

SMART steps

ONE: Consider light control and privacy. Are you looking for daytime control, nighttime control, or both? Do you want maximum light during the day but complete privacy at night? Will the shade have to accomplish these objectives alone, or are you pairing it with other elements that can help out? For example, you can combine a light-filtering shade that gives sun protection in the daytime with draperies that can be closed for privacy in the evening. Some roller shades and pleated shades can be installed bottom-up, covering the lower portion for all-day privacy while admitting light above.

If frequent adjustment is necessary, how easy is the operating mechanism? This may depend on the age and manual dexterity of the user. While adults find roller shades easy to adjust, small children often have problems.

TWO: Decide how you want the treatment mounted. Shades can be mounted inside or outside the window frame. Your decision can be a purely aesthetic one, or it can have some prac-

Left: Mixing the soft texture of a fabric valance with hard flat-fold bamboo shades adds interest to this window.

Installation Styles

Inside Mount

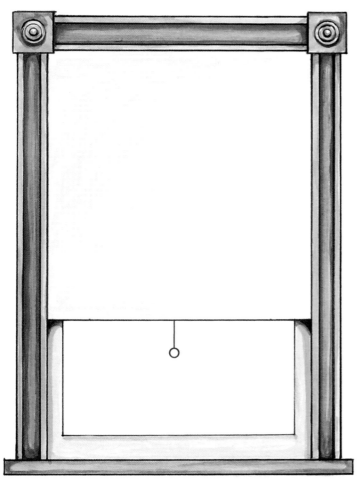

Outside Mount

tical reasons behind it. An *inside mount* is generally used if the shade will be paired with a top treatment, such as a valance or a swag, or with a treatment that would interfere with its operation, such as drawn curtains. It is also used if the window has a particularly handsome frame that you would like to show off or if there isn't enough room outside the window frame for the operating mechanism. From a design point of view, an inside mount permits the window frame to outline the treatment, giving it visual emphasis.

An *outside mount* is used if you want to conceal the window frame, camouflage the size of the the window, or simply leave a larger expanse of window treatment on view.

THREE: Choose a shade style. There are many different styles of shades. Some have their own intrinsic decorative character, while others are more chameleon-like, depending on fabric and trimming. For example, cellular shades and pleated shades (page 83) have a contemporary appearance. Because the fabric is gathered, balloon shades, cloud shades, and Austrian shades (pages 86-87) have a softer, dressmaker ambiance.

Roller shades, Roman shades, and cascade shades (pages 84-85) can easily change their personalities. When solids and geometrics are employed, they tend to have a more tailored air than when florals and laces are the chosen fabrics.

Scalloped and Curved Hems

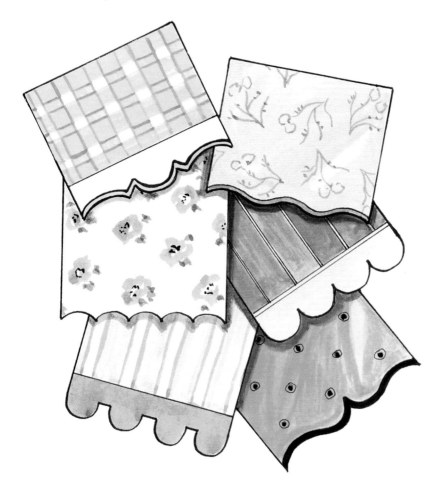

FOUR: Consider a hem design. Hems can be plain or intricate. But not all shades offer the same creative hemline opportunities. Pleated shades and cellular shades do not lend themselves to fancy hems.

Roller shades, however, are the perfect canvas for a variety of hem treatments. Decoratively shaped options include scalloped, curved, geometric, and notched hems. Instead of a conventional shade pull, roller shades can have a double layer at the lower edge that is notched so that a rod can be inserted through the hemline, creating an openwork design with a stable base. These edge treatments can mirror a pattern or motif found elsewhere in the room.

Decorative trims, including fringe, cording, ruffles, lace edgings, ribbon, and rickrack, can dress up the hemline of shades with cording mechanisms, such as balloon shades, cloud shades, and Austrian shades. Shades that tie, such as roll-up shades, usually have a plain hem because an embellished one would interfere with the shade's operation.

You may already have set ideas about the kind of finishing detail you want, or you may put this decision on hold until you have further explored the attributes of each individual type of shade. If you need to learn more, the information about shades on the following pages will help you reach the right decision.

Geometric and Notched Hems

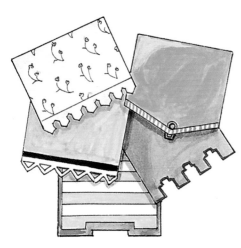

Rod and Notched Hems

Fringed, Corded, and Ruffled Hems

Pleated Shades

Pleated shades are a soft alternative to traditional blinds with the additional benefit of diffusing light. They come in many configurations, including ones for round, arched, and elliptical windows. Because one large shade is difficult to adjust, wide windows generally require two or more shades.

Special options include a double-cord control that allows you to move the shade in two directions—from the bottom up and from the top down (see below). Also, a track system with a split headrail makes it possible for two shades to operate on the same track. This feature is handy if you need two different types of shades, such as one for privacy or sun-filtering and one for color or style.

Basic Pleated Shade. A pleated shade is made of permanently folded paper or fabric. This type of shade stacks compactly—for instance, a 6-foot-long shade can pull back to under 3 inches. Pleats usually run as wide as 1 to $1^5/_8$ inches. Some fabric shades have a backing layer that offers high-energy efficiency, complete control of light, and privacy. Plus, they create a uniform appearance from outside the house.

Cellular Shades. A cellular shade is made of two or more layers of folded fabric, which create honeycomb-like "cells." (See right.) Cellular shades offer a number of benefits, ranging from UV protection to privacy control to insulative qualities. Stationary versions can be made for special window shapes, such as arches and ovals.

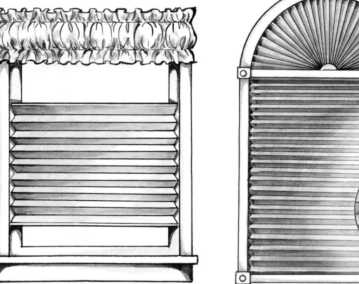

Pleated Shade

Cellular Shade

Below: A cellular "honeycomb" shade may be an affordable solution to a the problem of a drafty old window.

Basic and Batten Shades

Basic and batten shades are those that, when lowered, present a smooth surface against the window. This category includes roller shades (firm shades that can be made from fabric or vinyl), roll-up shades, fan shades, cascade shades (soft, stationary shades that have a distinctive draped effect when they are raised), and Roman shades (which are relatively firm and usually made from fabric).

Roller Shade. Roller shades can be purely functional or highly decorative. They're particularly good for small windows where you want to take advantage of the light. Generally, a roller shade is operated by a spring mechanism that is activated by tugging at the lower edge. This lower edge can be plain or embellished in any number of ways. A decorative pull (handle) can also be added to prevent wear on the lower edge of the shade.

The shade itself is made from vinyl or a tightly woven fabric. The fabric is either laminated (glued) to a backing or treated with a stiffening agent to give it firmer body. You can purchase roller shades in a variety of colors (usually neutrals and pastels), textures, and finishes. You can also have shades custom-made to match or complement fabric used elsewhere in the room. And you can make your own shades, using your own fabric. Kits are available that contain a roller with a built-in winding mechanism, brackets, wood batten (bottom slat), and

Fan Shade

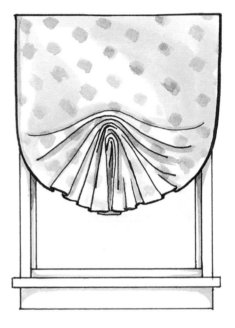

Roll-Up Shade

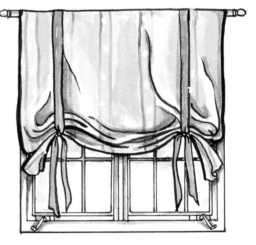

Opposite: A shaped or trimmed edge treatment can make a relaxed Roman shade something special.

Left: The stacking height of a shade is important if you want an unobstructed view when the shade is drawn up.

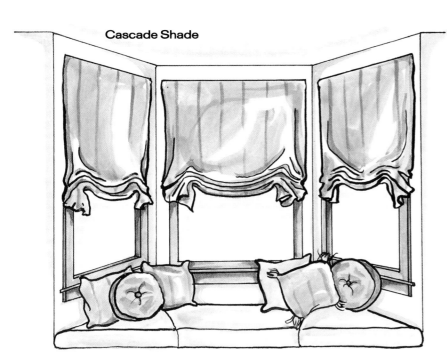

Cascade Shade

hardware. To stiffen the fabric, treat it first with a special liquid or spray stiffener, or apply an iron-on backing designed specifically for shades.

Roll-Up Shade. A roll-up shade, sometimes called a tied shade, is stationary. If it hangs from a pole or a shelf mounted outside the window frame, there should be enough room on the wall on both sides of the window to install the brackets. Once the shade is hung, the bottom part is rolled up to the desired position and secured with ties. The shade can be designed so that the lower edge folds into a soft swag when tied, or the lower edge can be reinforced with a batten. It needs a fabric that isn't too heavy but will stay in place, such as a silk taffeta. Strong, bold patterns work well on this particular type of shade. For visual punch, use contrasting ties.

Cascade Shade. Similar to a roll-up shade, a cascade shade usually has two sets of rings and cords sewn in a vertical arrangement onto the back of the shade. When the cords are pulled up, the sides swing in, giving it a scooped shape. To stabilize the shade, a rod can be inserted along the lower edge, centered between the rings. This shade is usually unlined.

Fan Shade. Another type of stationary shade, a fan shade has a single set of rings and cords that raises the center of the shade. This causes the sides to swing down, creating fan-shaped folds. Two battens, inserted along the hemline and meeting at the center, stabilize the shape. It looks best in plain and small-patterned fabrics, and it has a more formal appearance than other fabric shades.

Roman Shade. Unlike roll-up and fan shades, a Roman shade is a fabric shade that can be raised or lowered at will. When raised, it folds up evenly at regular intervals. These folds are created by a system of rings, cords, and precisely spaced horizontal battens. It is not hung on a rod. Instead, a Roman shade is mounted on a board that is attached inside the window frame or on the wall above the frame to let in full light.

This versatile treatment can be lined and insulated or made from a single layer of sheer fabric. A Roman shade can be designed so that it is smooth when lowered or has small, overlapping folds. A fold should never be more than 8 inches wide because the shade will not pull up evenly and the battens will bend. For wide windows, use multiple shades.

Festoon Shades

Festoon shades are gathered fabric shades that add softness and femininity to a room. They are designed to be raised or lowered by means of a ring-and-cord system that is attached to the back of the shade. When extended full length, festoons look like a gathered and scalloped curtain. When drawn up, they get fuller, poufed-up edges.

The amount of fullness—or pouf—can be controlled by the placement of the cords and rings. Wide spaces between them means shallower scallops. Narrower spaces mean deeper scallops. It is not necessary for all the scallops to be the same width. For example, a festoon could have a wide scallop in the center and narrow ones at the ends.

Balloon Shade. A balloon shade is gathered in scallops across the width of the shade and is raised in soft folds by a

Balloon Shade

Tailed Balloon Shade

cording system. Although it can be designed with one scoop, a balloon shade is typically three to four scallops wide and has an inverted-pleat heading.

The result is a slightly tailored shade with ruching that falls only along the scallops. When lowered to floor or sill level, a balloon shade looks like a full-length curtain. However, if you prefer the scalloped shape, increase the length of the fabric so that the ruching remains even when the shade is completely lowered. To accent the shape of the hem, add ruffles or fringe. (Smaller details, such as cording, won't show up.) Another hem option is called skirting. Leaving off the bottom rings creates a flat panel, over which the scallops fall.

Choose fabrics in solid colors or simple patterns for balloon shades. Stripes, checks, plaids, miniprints,

and small-scale florals work well, but bolder patterns may look excessive and may be distorted by the ruching.

Tailed Balloon Shade. By omitting the side cords on a balloon shade, a tail is created. Tails can be just a few inches long or dramatic drops that are double the width of the scallop. Long tails look best with shades that are only one or two scallops wide. Shorter tails are better when there are multiple scoops. A contrast binding along the lower edge or sides accentuates the shape.

Cloud Shade. When a balloon shade has a gathered or pleated heading, such as a pencil pleat, it is often referred to as a cloud shade. A cloud shade has a scalloped hem and exuberant ruching, which results in a very feminine treatment. The lower edge is usually left plain or trimmed with a deep ruffle; a narrow trim would simply get lost in the billowy edge.

Austrian Shade. The full fabric length is at least double the drop in an Austrian shade. As a result, even when the shade is completely lowered, horizontal scallops remain. Often made from a sheer or lacy fabric, it looks great alone or as an undercurtain for heavy draperies.

Opposite: Pleated balloon shades have only one or two scoops at the bottom. The heading is straight , and there is less fullness to the overall width.

Above: An Austrian shade is best when it is made from a translucent fabric. Paired with curtains, the completed look is formal.

Skirted Balloon Shade

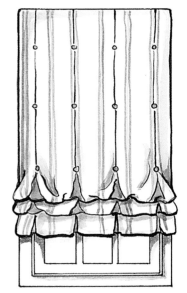

Cloud Shade

BLINDS

Blinds encompass a group of hard window treatments composed of movable slats. Blinds can be raised and lowered; many versions can also be opened and closed to permit varying degrees of light to enter the room. They have a linear quality that is compatible with tailored and contemporary interiors. For a traditional decor, blinds are usually combined with curtains for a softening effect.

Above: Blinds are a great way to create a multilayer look on a window. Here, blinds are paired with a scalloped valance to coordinate the window with the traditional style of the room.

MATERIALS

Slats are made from a variety of materials that are generally firm or rigid in nature. These slats are strung together so that they can be rolled up, usually on a spring mechanism, or pulled up with a cord.

■ **Paper**. Paper blinds are pleated so that the creases remain even when the blinds are down. They are easy to dust, inexpensive, and available in a wide range of colors. Optional metallic backing repels the sun in the summer.

■ **Cane.** Whole or split cane, such as bamboo or rattan, is used for blinds that roll up or fold into pleats. Small spaces between the slats let through some light, which makes blinds made from this material translucent from inside and outside the room.

■ **Metal.** Aluminum alloy is the traditional material for Venetian blinds, which have slats that are slightly curved. They come in a variety of widths, from ½ to 2 inches wide, and can be custom-fit for special-shaped windows or cut to fit around air conditioners.

■ **Wood.** For Venetian blinds, wooden slats are 1 to 2 inches wide. Tapes or thin cords control the movement. Adjusting the angles of the slats controls the amount of light. The slats can be stained or painted. They offer a natural look, durability, and insulating properties. Woven cloth tapes are available with wood-slat blinds in coordinating or contrasting colors. Narrow strips of wood are also used for woven blinds.

■ **Plastic or Vinyl.** Plastic or vinyl 1-inch slats function the same as wood or aluminum versions but are less expensive. Aside from a range of colors, options include high-gloss and pearlized finishes.

■ **Fabric.** Stiffened, textured fabric is often used for vertical blinds. For specialty blinds, fabric slats form an interior layer that is sandwiched between two sheer facings. The sheer fabric softens the hard lines of traditional blinds. Plus, when open, it lets light filter into the room and provides some degree of privacy.

Woven Blinds

As a category, woven blinds tend to be informal in style and contribute to the casual, outdoor feeling of a room. They are good for family rooms, sunrooms, and porches, but they also show up in kitchens and bathrooms. Woven blinds come in standard sizes and are composed of inexpensive materials, making them the most reasonably priced option when compared with other types of blinds.

To create these blinds, narrow horizontal slats are woven together using strips of cotton twine. Woven blinds may be mounted inside the window with screw-and-eye hangers. A pulley system pulls the blinds up. They can be fixed at any level by winding the cord around a cleat that is attached to the wall. Use them alone or with a top treatment.

Matchstick Blinds. Made from very thin strips of natural fibers, matchstick blinds are usually cane or basswood. A matchstick blind can be stained, painted, or left natural. It filters the light during the day, but because there are spaces between the slats, it does not offer complete privacy during the day or night.

Plastic Blinds. Similar to a matchstick blind, a plastic blind is constructed from narrow plastic slats, called quills, with closely spaced strips of twine. It comes in white and a wide range of colors. Plastic blinds are somewhat less bulky than matchstick blinds.

Right: These natural blinds filter strong early morning light while keeping the room bright.

Matchstick Blind

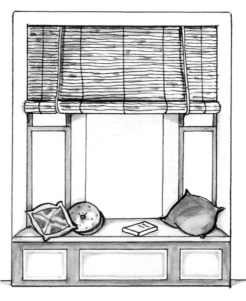

Plastic Blind

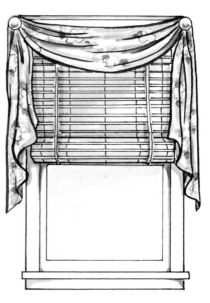

Horizontal and Vertical Blinds

Traditional slatted blinds come in a wide variety of materials and finishes. Used alone, they have a linear, almost industrial quality that works well in a contemporary setting. However, it is easy to warm up blinds by pairing them with curtains or any of the fabric top treatments.

Venetian Blind. Usually made from aluminum, the venetian blind consists of a series of 1-, 2-, or 3-inch-wide horizontal slats held together by cords and twill tapes. The slats can be raised, lowered, or angled to control light. It comes in many colors and finishes, including anti-static, metallic, pearl, suede, and a perforated finish that permits light to enter even when the blind is closed.

Wood-Slat Blind. A Venetian blind constructed from wood is called a wood-slat blind. The finish can be natural, stained, or painted. Because wood slats are thicker, wood blinds have a deeper stack than that of aluminum when pulled up. When down, this blind is reminiscent of shutters, particularly when the slats are in the closed position.

Miniblind. Narrow, 1/2-inch-wide aluminum or PVC Venetian blinds are called miniblinds. They are particularly popular because when the blind is lowered and fully open, the slats are almost invisible. They come in a wide range of colors to match almost any decor. The 1-inch-wide blinds are also sometimes referred to as miniblinds.

Vertical Blind. Although vertical blinds are especially popular in offices, they are equally at home in a contemporary residential setting. They are installed on a track across the top of the window so that they can be drawn closed, just like draperies. Remote-control mechanisms are available so that they don't have to be closed by hand. The slats can be linked together at the bottom by a metal chain or left hanging free. The slats are commonly made from wood, synthetic flexible material, or stiffened fabric. Special track systems are available for bow, bay, and angled windows.

Window Shading. A special type of blind, called a window shading, features soft fabric slats inserted between two layers of sheer fabric, allowing daylight to filter through the open slats. Window shadings are available in horizontal and vertical styles. The fabric on the horizontal blinds lies flat; the vertical version falls in soft folds like pleated drapery. This can be an alternative to a vertical blind if you prefer the look of something softer than a blind but more structured than a lightweight curtain.

Below: Vertical blinds have a sleek, modern appearance, so they look their best used alone in a contemporary setting.

Opposite: Blinds can be a practical option for the bathroom because they offer privacy when the slats are closed and ventilation when they're open.

Wood-Slat Blind

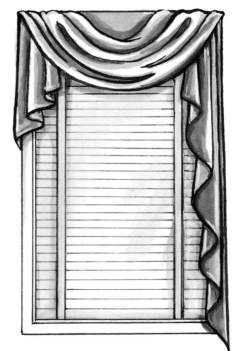

Vertical Blind

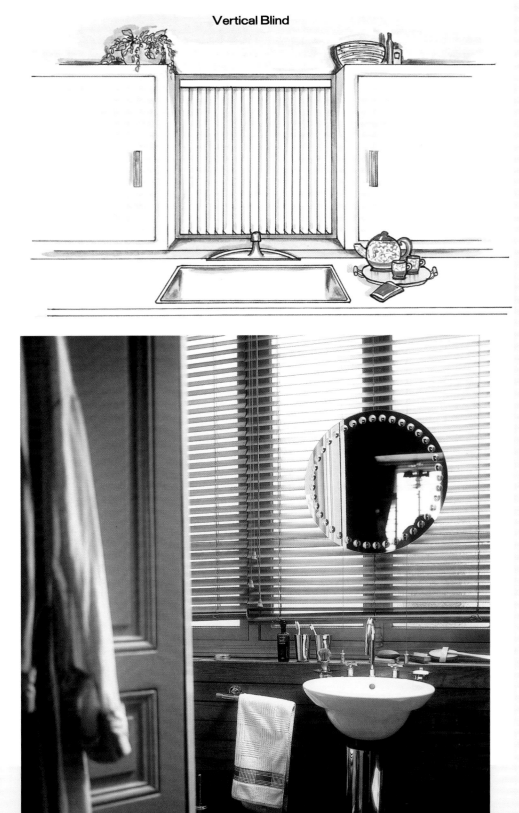

Miniblind

SHUTTERS

Shutters conjure images of cozy interiors that envelop you in warmth and comfort. They can be installed inside the window frame on a mounting strip or outside the window opening in a frame of their own. Depending on the size of the window, they can be installed as a single shutter that swings open to one side of the window, as a pair that opens in the center, or as four or more panels that are hinged together and split at the center.

Shutters offer various options for privacy. Because they are good companions to almost any top treatment, they can be installed to cover the lower half of the window only. They are also a good buffer against noise, which makes them popular for street-level rooms in urban areas. When a window has two or more sets of shutters, a divider rail can be installed so that the top half can open separately from the bottom.

As a general rule, use the minimum number of panels possible to achieve the desired effect. More panels mean that more of the window is covered by the frames. Fewer panels will give you the most unobstructed view and allow you to control the light better.

Louvers are the vertical and horizontal slats that give shutters their character. Standard louver widths are $1\frac{1}{4}$, $1\frac{3}{4}$, $2\frac{1}{2}$, $3\frac{1}{2}$, and $4\frac{1}{2}$ inches. Wider louvers allow more sunlight into a room; narrow slats provide more screening.

MATERIALS

There are two materials that are used to make louvered and paneled shutters: wood and vinyl polymer.

■ **Wood.** Shutters are usually made of pine. Unfinished wood shutters can be stained or painted any color; some styles are available prepainted in standard and custom colors. Wood shutters are a durable investment that enhances a home's value.

■ **Vinyl.** Vinyl polymer solves the problem presented by wood: warping in bathrooms and other areas where there is steam and moisture. This material also wipes clean easily.

Opposite: Shutters can be stacked on large banks of windows. This arrangement suits this traditional bedroom.

Right: Louvered plantation shutters are popular today. Here, they update the look of the entire room.

SMARTtip　　Shutters

For the maximum the amount of light coming through shutters, use the largest panel possible on the window. Make sure the shutters have the same number of louvers per panel so that all of the windows in the room look unified. However, don't choose a panel that is over 48 inches high, because the shutter becomes unwieldy. Also, any window that is wider than 96 inches requires extra support framing.

Louver Shutters

There are three basic types of louver shutters: plantation, vertical, and café. If these don't suit your exact needs, be aware that shutters can be custom-fitted to specialty shaped windows, such as arches. With most of these configurations, louvers will not be movable.

Plantation Shutter. A shutter with a generous proportion is called a plantation shutter. For this style, the louvers are generally $2\frac{1}{2}$ to $4\frac{1}{2}$ inches wide and are set into panels that are 15 to 36 inches wide. Plantation shutters are frequently used in multiple sets, covering the entire window from top to bottom. These attractive shutters are also frequently used alone without any other window treatment. They can be installed as sliding panels, too. This is an arrangement that is suited to floor-length windows.

Vertical-Louver Shutter. A vertical-louver shutter is a traditional type with louvers generally $1\frac{1}{4}$ inches wide and set in panels 8 to 12 inches wide. If you wish to mount it inside the window frame, you need a 2-inch clearance between the face of the window and the back of the shutter so that the louvers can open freely. If the distance is less than 2 inches, an outside mount will be required.

Café Shutter. Café refers to the type of installation, rather than the style of the shutter. Like a café curtain, it is installed to cover half of the window. It can cover the lower half only, or a set can be double hung to cover the upper and lower halves of a window.

Café Shutters

Vertical-Louver Shutters

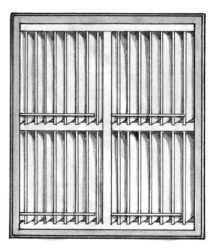

Left: Wooden shutters are classic. They bring another strong architectural feature to a home. They can be standard or custom-fit.

More Shutter Styles

Strictly speaking, shutters can be any type of movable window covering that is set into a frame—a panel shutter is the most classic example of this. A fabric-insert shutter and a Shoji screen are other variations. No light passes through a closed panel shutter. However, a fabric-insert shutter or a Shoji screen diffuses light when closed.

Panel Shutter. A panel shutter consists of solid pieces of wood or interlocking strips of wood. It usually has some type of decoration, such as raised moldings.

Fabric-Insert Shutter. Consisting of panels of gathered fabric set into a wood frame, a fabric-insert shutter can be used to create a more colorful look than that of traditional shutters. The fabric can be printed or plain, solid or lace; it can be selected to match the wallpaper or to repeat a fabric used elsewhere in the room. The best choices are light- to medium-weight fabrics that gather easily. An unlined fabric panel can be damaged by sun, so choose a sun-resistant fabric.

Shoji Screen. A shoji screen consists of a translucent panel set into a delicate wood frame. It usually slides open on a track, but it can also be hinged to work like a shutter. Often used as doors, shoji screens are also appropriate for windows. In traditional Japanese homes, the panels were originally made from rice paper. Today, panels are made from durable synthetic materials. This covering is compatible with both contemporary and Asian decor.

Right: A custom-designed shoji screen makes an attractive minimalist treatment for windows or patio doors.

Shoji Screen

a gallery of...

1 In a period home, solid-panel shutters fold back into the frame of the window.

2 Roll-up matchstick blinds , wicker furniture, and a palm tree turn a windowed bay into a exotic getaway.

3 Louvered shutters let you play with natural light.

4 Plain fabric shades can be unobtrusive on garden windows.

5 Patterned fabric shades can add personality to a space.

6 Operable shutters are an option for a window above the tub.

7 Wooden shutters can be stained to match cabinets or other furniture or woodwork.

...smart ideas

1 A tassle hangs from a curtain pin and punctuates the V hemline of this flat Roman shade.

2 Cords threaded through a series of grommets are used to operate this relaxed version of a Roman shade.

3 A button tab heading and a fringed hem dress up this design.

4 A balloon shade fabricated in silk looks elegant.

5 Bottom-mounted shades can be adjusted to meet any need.

6 Practical blinds and shades can be paired with curtains for a softer, dressier appearance.

7 A vertical-stripe fabric adds a tailored note to double-scoop balloon shades.

2

3

5

4

6

7

CHAPTER 7

TOP TREATMENTS

**SWAGS AND JABOTS ■ VALANCES ■
STRUCTURED SWAGS ■ SCARF SWAGS
CORNICES ■ BALLOON VALANCES ■
PLEATED VALANCES ■ TABBED
VALANCES ■ GATHERED VALANCES ■
SHAPED CORNICES ■ BOX CORNICES ■
LAMBREQUINS**

Originally, top treatments were more practical than decorative. They provided an added layer of insulation over drafty windows. As more fabrics and dyes became available, cornices, valances, and swags became stylish and contributed to the overall aesthetic appeal of complex window-treatment designs. Today, they can be used for numerous decorative purposes. For example, ruffled valances can soften the look of hard treatments, such as shutters; a padded box cornice can complement the tailored character of vertical blinds; and ornate swags can add drama to a plain paneled curtain. In general, any top treatment provides another opportunity for creating variety in form, pattern, or color. Used alone, a cornice, valance, or swag can be fashionable without obstructing the view or blocking the light.

Top treatments can also hide unsightly hardware and camouflage imperfect curtain headings. Plus, by installing a top treatment high on the wall above a poorly proportioned window, you can improve the appearance of the window. With the exception of a cornice, you can position a top treatment inside or outside of the window frame, depending on the available wall space. Look for other ways to make it distinctive—with coordinating or contrasting colors as well as special ornaments or trimmings.

SWAGS & JABOTS

Swags and jabots are purely decorative window treatments. We tend to think of them as gracing tall windows in stately country homes and elegant town houses, but they can be a beautiful addition to any room. Heavy fabrics, such as brocades and velvets, and elaborate trimmings are in keeping with their original formality. However, making them with lighter fabrics and simpler trimmings, as well as mating them with shutters or blinds, produces a less formal look.

Swags are the scallop-like shapes that extend across the top of the window. *Jabots* are the tails—softly pleated or shaped side panels with symmetrical or asymmetrical hemlines that flank a swag.

SMART steps

ONE Choose a symmetrical or asymmetrical arrangement. In a symmetrical arrangement, the window treatment is the same on both sides of an imagined or real centerline. An example of a symmetrical arrangement is a series of three swags with matching jabots framing a picture window. The middle swag is positioned so that its center is exactly at the center of the window; one swag and one jabot flank it on each side. Because a symmetrical treatment appears formal, it looks appropriate in a traditional setting.

An asymmetrical arrangement refers to the balance between different-sized elements of a window treatment as a result of placement. For instance, a circular window can be dressed with a swag that has a long jabot (tail) on one side and a short one on the other. As long as the scale of the treatment is correct, the results will be quite pleasing.

Because an asymmetrical arrangement appears informal, it looks at home in a contemporary setting. But it can also work well in a traditional setting. Imagine a wall with a fireplace and two windows which are equal in size and distance from the fireplace. Each window could have a short jabot on its inside edge and a longer one on its outside edge. Individually, each window arrangement is asymmetrical. However, because they are mirror images of each other, the overall result is formal and symmetrical.

TWO Determine the number of swags that your window needs. The size of the window affects how many swags are needed. As a general guideline, swags should be no more than 40 inches wide. The depth (or drop) of each swag generally ranges from 12 to 20 inches, depending on the height of the window.

Narrower windows look better with one or two swags. With more, the window treatment will look crowded. The swags should overlap slightly. If the swags are paired with a curtain or a blind, they should overlap enough to conceal the headings underneath. Wide windows require multiple swags

Opposite: A swag valance has a sweeping effect across the top of a window. In this case, each scoop is attached to the wall by hardware that is hidden behind a maltese cross.

Below: A swag-and-jabot valance that is draped over a rod should be carefully arranged so that the scoops are evenly spaced without looking crowded.

to match their generous proportions. It is usually more attractive to use an uneven number of swags so that one full swag falls at the center of the window.

To help you decide how many swags you need, draw your window to scale on a piece of paper. Using tissue-paper overlays, sketch different arrangements of swags. When you find a pleasing one, drape lengths of string or cloth measuring tape across the top of your window to mimic the desired effect.

THREE Decide between formal and informal styles. This depends on several factors: the room's decor, the look you want to achieve, and the style of your curtains. Formal versions of swags and jabots are mounted on a board that is attached to the wall or the window frame. They are usually made from mid- to heavyweight fabrics, such as velvet, brocade, or satin, and they are lined. Trimmings, including tassels and braids, can be opulent. Formal swags and jabots are usually paired with curtains and, sometimes, sheer inner curtains. Informal versions tend to be made from mid- to light-weight fabrics, such as chintz, linen, or voile. They often serve as top treatments for blinds and shutters. Informal swags and jabots may be mounted on a board but can also be hung from rods. Trimmings are

applied with a light touch. Some informal swags are unlined and resemble scarves casually tossed over a pole.

VALANCES

Valance is an all-encompassing term used for a range of treatments that are designed to be purely decorative. It is a soft fabric treatment, one that is usually draped, gathered, or folded. It covers no more than the upper third of the window glass, and generally covers much less. Valances can

(*Text continued on page 108*)

Structured Swags

Although a swag-and-jabot arrangement looks as though it is made from one piece of material, each element is actually a series of separate sections. A swag can have a deep or a shallow drop. The deeper the drop, the fuller the folds.

A fan swag, which has folds that radiate out from the top center, is a variation of the traditional swag. Swags and jabots can also be hung on a rod with rings to form an apron-like effect over side curtains. Another variation foregoes the mounting board in favor of hidden hardware installed at the top of each jabot. This can create a crown-like design above a French door where there are unusually high ceilings, or it can enhance the illusion of a taller window.

Jabots are the tails of fabric that complement the swags. There is generally a jabot at each end of the treatment. However, for more visual interest, the treatment can also be designed with alternating swags and jabots. Plus, the jabot can lie under or over the ends of the swag.

Jabots are usually lined because the added weight helps them to hang better. If the underside of the tails is visible, a contrast lining is often used to accentuate the shape of the design.

The most common jabot style is the cascade, an asymmetrical tail that is created by fan-folding the fabric. When all the folds are arranged exactly on top of each other, the jabot falls in a narrow, stacked pattern. When the folds are staggered, the jabot is wider and the hemline undulates upwards. The other common asymmetrical tail is the spiral—a corkscrew-like arrangement. Asymmetrical jabots are used in mirror-image at the ends of the treatment.

Symmetrical jabot styles include the fluted jabot, an open tube that curls to the underside, and the pipe jabot, a closed tube with a pointed hem. Symmetrical jabots are used at the center of the window, between the swags. They also can be used at each end in place of an asymmetrical tail.

Trimmings pair naturally with swags and jabots. The deep scoops of the swags and the undulating edges of the jabots often feature bullion and pom-pom fringe, cording, and ribbon borders. Rosettes, choux (ruched rosettes), Maltese crosses, and tassels can be added at the point where the swag is attached to the jabot.

Swag on Curtain Rings

Fan Swag

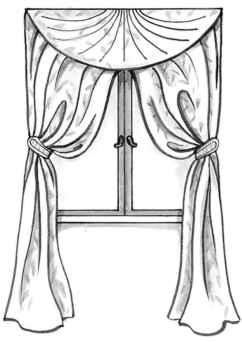

Triple Swag and Cascade Jabot

Swag on Curtain Hold Backs

Opposite: A matching box valance cleverly conceals the hardware mounting for the swags and jabots.

Above: This layered look features a swag valance that is tied to a painted pole. The pole, which is visible, becomes part of the design.

Cascade Jabot

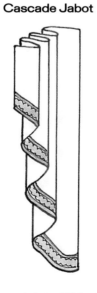

Spiral

Fluted Jabot

Pipe Jabot

Scarf Swags

Scarf swags are a more relaxed interpretation of the swag-and-jabot treatment. They can be short, meaning sill length or shorter, or long, to the floor or gracefully puddling. Generally, a scarf treatment is created from one long piece of fabric. Lightweight fabrics with no right or wrong side, such as batiste, voile, lace, linen, and lawn, are good choices because these fabrics fall into the soft folds that make scarf swags attractive yet informal.

Scarf treatments can be wrapped over poles; suspended from brackets, hold backs, or rings; or tacked up with decorative hardware. Special brackets are also available to secure the fabric into various swag, tail, and rosette formations while remaining completely hidden from sight.

Scarf swags that are sill-length or shorter require some care to establish pleasing proportions. If the scarf is used alone, the tails should extend at least one-third of the way down the window. Otherwise, the end product tends to look a bit skimpy. Short scarves can also be installed over floor-length curtains to add drama to the window.

When a floor-length scarf is hung over a curtain rod, it is often referred to as a draped pole. These treatments can be tricky to hang simply because they use so much fabric. Puddling solves the problem of getting the hemline just right. Because they are heavier, long scarves also require more support than a short treatment. An asymmetrical style can be an interesting counterpoint to a window with an unusual shape.

Crisscrossed Draped Pole

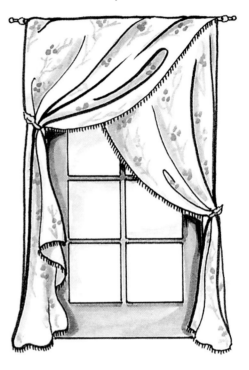

Wrapped Draped Pole

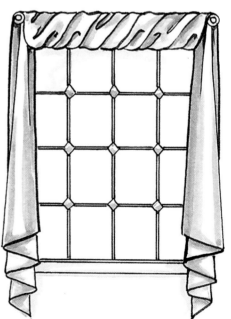

Scarf Swag on Brackets

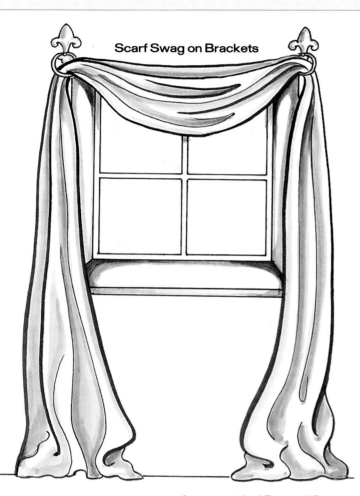

Asymmetrical Draped Swag

Double Scarf Swag

Opposite: Fabric can be twisted and draped around a pole to create a tight swagged effect.

Above: A fishtail scarf swag is a length of fabric that is left to drape loosely over the sides of the window frame.

(Continued from page 103)
take many forms—from simple bands of fabric to elaborate arrangements with gathers and pleats. A valance can accompany drapery or stand alone.

While a valance does not contribute to privacy or light-blockage (except minimally), it does provide a way to add color and interest to a window, visually balance curtains or shutters below, and add another layer of decoration that can be enhanced by cords, gathers, pleats, and trim. From a practical point of view, it hides any unattractive hardware that belongs to underneath treatments, such as plain curtain rods and shade rollers. It also softens hard treatments, such as wood or metal blinds.

Proper Proportions. The valance should be in proportion to the window. This means that it should not be so long that it blocks the light or so short that it looks like a skimpy afterthought on the window. Longer windows mean longer valances. Valances are generally between 10 and 16 inches long, including the heading and any trim at the lower edge. Valances that involve generous swoops and folds of fabric, such as some variations of the balloon valance, may be a little longer to accommodate the abundance of fabric. Valance tails should fall one-third of the way down the window.

Several other factors will influence the proportions of your valance. For an outside mount, the valance should be longer so that it extends to a pleasing point on the window glass. For an inside mount, the valance will be shorter. If your window has mullions or defined panes, avoid having the lower edge of the valance fall just short of a horizontal bar. The result will be an unattractive, chopped-off look. If the valance is installed over floor-length curtains, it should be longer so that it is in proportion to the expanse of fabric underneath. In this scenario, a valance with tails could be a dramatic topper extending one-third of the way down the draperies at the sides of the window.

Styles. A valance can be pleated, gathered, shirred, or smooth. The fabric can match the rest of the window dressing, introduce a note of contrast, or repeat a fabric or color used elsewhere in the room. It can be hung on a decorative rod or a plain rod. The lower edge of the valance can be treated in a number of ways: it can be shaped, trimmed

SMARTtip · Sizing a Valance

To determine the most pleasing proportion for your valance before making any purchases, try the brown-paper template technique. Cut some grocery bags apart or purchase brown kraft paper. Draw a template equal to the right length and outline shape of your proposed valance. Cut out the template, and tape it in place across the top of your window. Analyze the proportions of the template. Is it too long? Too short? Make any necessary adjustments, and then note the final measurements.

Left: Although a box-pleated valance is tailored, it doesn't have to look severe, especially if it's fabricated in a floral print. This style pairs well with plain panels.

Above: Some valances can be decorative used alone. In this cottage-style room, a tabbed valance is suspended from finials in a casual and slightly whimsical way.

with a contrasting band, fringed, or adorned with a decorative edging, such as lace or braid. It can be longer at the sides than at the center. The upper edge can have looped cords, rosettes, bows, or tassels. These details, too, can be echoed elsewhere in the room, such as on a pillow.

For durability and to ensure that they hang properly, many valances are lined. However, light and breezy styles, such as those made from lace, voile, or other semitransparent fabrics, are not lined. A lining can also be eliminated if the valance is made from a particularly crisp fabric such as chintz or taffeta.

When selecting a valance, choose a style that is compatible with your overall decor. For example, a gathered valance would look out of place in a contemporary setting, whereas a pleated or geometrically shaped one might be an excellent choice. Many pleated valances work well in formal settings,

while balloon valances are frequently a good choice in a Victorian decor.

Hardware. The hardware for valances is as diversified as that for curtains. In some cases, the hardware and the style of the valance work together to create the overall effect. Decorative rods are a particularly good choice for tabbed valances. Clear rods are available for near-invisible hanging of lace and sheer valances. Double rods mean only one set of hardware for valance and draperies. Triple rods can accommodate an inner curtain, too. Some rods, such as wide continental rods and those with arched tops, actually create the shape of the valance. Install the valance rod so that the sides of the valance extend slightly beyond any underneath treatment.

CORNICES

Although cornices and valances are often mistaken for each other, a *cornice* is a more permanent arrangement. In fact, some cornices are elaborate wood structures that look like architectural elements. Others are upholstered or otherwise

(Text continued on page 114)

Balloon Valances

A balloon valance gets its name from the fact that it has a full, puffed-out shape. Alone, it imparts a soft, somewhat feminine look to a window. In appearance, the basic balloon valance looks like a shorter version of the balloon shade, but it does not move up and down. Used with floor-length draperies, the effect is more formal. When designed with side tails, it has a tailored appearance.

A puff valance is a self-lined valance that is open at the ends so that the two layers can be pulled apart to form a pouf. The cloud valance is similar to the balloon valance but with more fullness at the lower edge of the scallops. The shirred Austrian has scallops from top to bottom.

Below: Balloon valances are popular in the kitchen because they look decorative without being cumbersome.

Tailed Balloon Valance

Balloon Valance

Puff Valance

Cloud Valance

Austrian Valance

Pleated Valances

A pleated valance has a tailored, dress-maker look. Any of the headings that are commonly used for drapery can be applied to a pleated valance. The simplest version is the box-pleat valance, which looks like a schoolgirl's crisply pleated skirt. Other versions, such as the triple-pleat and butterfly-pleat valances, are pleated at the top and then released into soft folds. For the pleated-and-gathered valance, the area below the pleats is gathered up so that a series of swag-and-jabot-like shapes are formed. The cartridge-pleat valance consists of groupings of narrow, rounded pleats, spaced at intervals across the valance. On the bell-pleat valance, the unpressed pleats form soft cones of fabric.

Right: Box pleats fold nicely into a good-quality cotton with body. The edging emphasizes the pleats' shape.

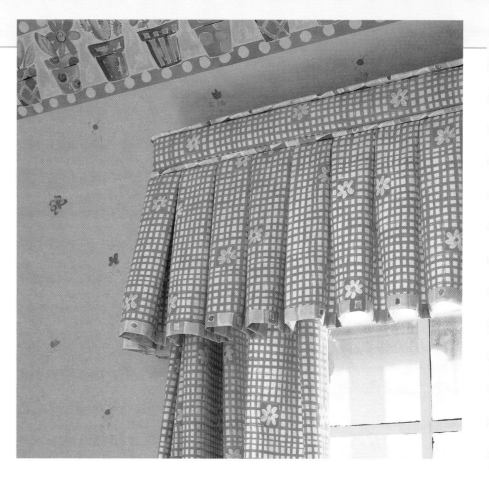

Box-Pleat Valance

Pleated and Gathered Valance

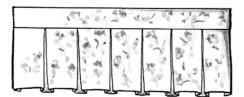

Cartridge-Pleat Valance

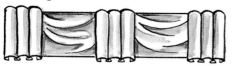

Triple-Pleat Valance

Butterfly-Pleat Valance

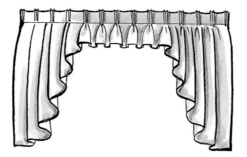

Bell-Pleat Valance

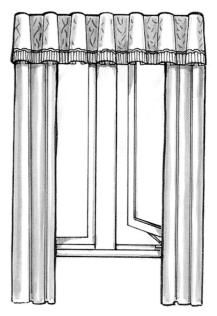

Tabbed Valances

With a tabbed valance, the drapery pole becomes an integral part of the window treatment. Because the tabs occur at intervals along the valance, this treatment is a wonderful way to showcase decorative rods and finials. (See Chapter 10, "Drapery Hardware," page 148.) Tabs can be made from wide or narrow strips of fabric, ribbon, or cord that complement or contrast with the main fabric of the curtain. They can also be left plain or decorated with details such as buttons, bows, and rosettes.

Hardware hangers, such as drapery rings or café clips, can substitute for the tabs. A flat valance, one that is the same width as the window, is called a banner valance. A fuller effect is created by selecting a valance that is at least one and a half times wider than the window.

Above: A crenellated banner valance's uncomplicated shape is in keeping with the simplicity of this old-fashioned bathroom.

Tabbed Valance

Rosette Valance

Scalloped Valance

Arched Valance

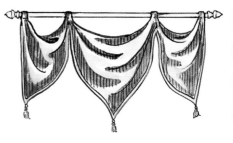

Bow Tie Valance

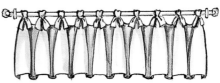

Gathered Valances

The basic gathered valance is a long flat valance with a rod pocket. When it is shirred up on the rod, the gathers form. Generally, the flat valance is two to three times the width of the window. When using large amounts of material, a light-weight fabric is better because it creates a fuller effect.

Specialized standard curtain rods, such as wide continental rods or arched rods, give the gathered valance a distinctive look. The Federal valance is created by pulling the ruffle up and securing it with a few stitches just below the rod pocket. Ruffled headers and shaped hemlines are another way to alter the look.

Federal Valance

Rod-Pocket Valance

Pointed Valance

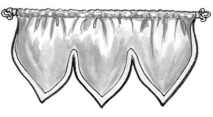

Arch-Top Valance

Right: Used alone on a window, a gathered valance with a scalloped hemline has a slightly dressier look.

Right and below: A cornice can be cut entirely out of wood and painted or upholstered. Here, composition ornament was added to the cornice box to make an architectural statement.

(Continued from page 108)
covered with fabric to coordinate with the decor of the room.

Materials. Traditionally, cornices were wooden boxes that were painted or covered with fabric. Painted cornices often featured molding to heighten the architectural look of the treatments. Today, cornices are also made from buckram or cardboard attached to a cornice shelf or from a sturdy material such as foam core. Although these materials are stiff, they are easier to cut into curved and geometric shapes, expanding the variety of cornice designs.

The conventional box cornice has four sides: a face board (the front), two end boards (the sides), and a dust board (the top). The dust board helps deflect drafts—one reason why wood cornices were so popular in older homes.

Wooden box cornices can be painted or stained to match other woodwork in the room. They also provide a mounting place for indirect lighting, which can dramatically highlight the window treatment. Fabric coverings on wooden or foam-core box cornices can be padded, tufted, pleated, and outlined with piping for an upholstered look. Cornice shelves can have fabric attached along the edges of the shelf, with or without face board and end boards.

Scale. A cornice should balance the treatment and be in scale with the window. Because of its architectural nature, a cornice is always mounted outside the window, usually with the dust board or shelf aligned with the top of the frame. The cornice should be tall enough to cover the window's upper frame, plus the hardware and headings of any treatments underneath. Generally, cornices are 12½ to 15 inches long. If the window is too short or the ceiling is very high, install the cornice on the wall above the window.

Cornices can be custom-made or purchased ready-made in standard sizes. Cornice kits are also available for easy assembly from lightweight panels of polystyrene; you supply the batting and the fabric.

Shaped Cornices

Although a shaped cornice can be constructed from a cornice box, most use a cornice shelf. Buckram or cardboard—both easier than wood for cutting elaborately shaped designs—is attached to the shelf, serving as firm face- and end-board surfaces to be covered with fabric. The lower edge of a shaped cornice follows a geometric pattern. Scallops, inverted scallops, notches, and S-curves are common motifs. Piping or bands of trim can be used to emphasize the shape. A series of overlapping shapes, such as the triangles of the pendant cornice, can be individually reinforced and then attached to the cornice shelf. The cornice shelf can also support a wood crown that extends above the shelf; a fabric ruffle is attached below it.

Right and below: To create this exotic shape, a template of the valance face can be cut from stiffened buckram.

Notched Cornice

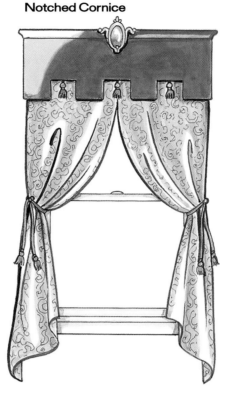

Shaped Cornice

Scalloped Cornice

Cutout Cornice

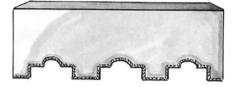

Geometric Cornice

Pendant Cornice

Wood Crown

Fabric-Insert Cornice

Box Cornices

A box cornice provides a solid base for a variety of coverings. In general, a box-based cornice has more visual weight then one with a shelf base. Stained or painted wood-box cornices are embellished with architectural details, such as crown moldings, picture moldings, and carvings. This style is particularly appropriate for large, formal rooms, and it is an effective cover for curtain rods, especially those that are high on a wall.

Upholstered box cornices are covered in mid- to heavy-weight fabrics. The fabric is applied over batting and can be pulled tautly and evenly to look smooth, or it can be manipulated into horizontal or vertical pleats. The upholstery can also be tufted with buttons or studs to give it interest. Sheers and lightweight fabrics are fine for hourglass, turban, smocked, swag, and other soft effects that are hung across the cornice.

Pleated Cornice

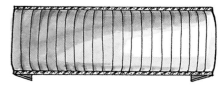

Swagged Cornice

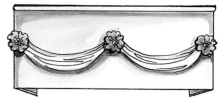

Right: Alternate-color squares of fabric have been positioned in a diamond pattern on the face of a box cornice.

Hourglass Cornice

Turban Cornice

Mock Roman Cornice

Wood Cornice

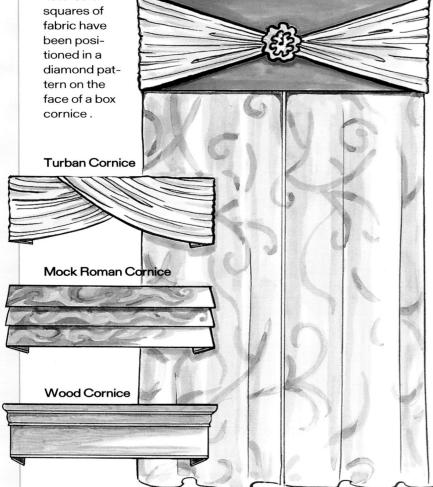

Lambrequins

According to its traditional definition, a lambrequin is another name for a valance or a cornice. Today, however, it has come to mean a three-sided frame installed around the window—essentially a cornice with sides that extend down at least two-thirds of the window or to the floor. From a practical point of view, a lambrequin can conceal an unattractive window frame and help block excessive drafts. It also adds formality to the room. Because the long sides of a lambrequin are subject to bumping and banging, a wood base, securely anchored to the window frame or wall, is best. A lambrequin can be upholstered, painted, or stained just like a box cornice. Moldings and painted details often echo other architectural details in the room.

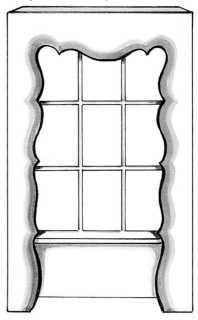

Arched Lambrequin

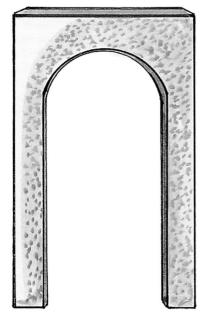

Tapered Lambrequin

Above: A lambrequin actually looks like an extended cornice. Here, a pair of lambrequins have been installed over simple sheers to heighten the impact of two modest windows.

Shaped Lambrequin

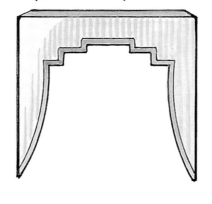

1

3

2

4

5

a gallery of...

1 A swag valance crowns a formal window treatment.

2 An upholstered box cornice has a tailored appearance.

3 A scalloped valance looks traditional.

4 A box-pleated valance looks soft but neat.

5 A pleated valance pairs with curtains.

6 A wisp of fabric creates a simple scarf swag.

7 Fabric draped over a pole falls into evenly spaced scallops.

8 A printed valance of pleats and gathers accents café curtains.

9 Points add a pretty dressmaker detail to this design.

1

4

2

5

3

1. A top treatment extends across a wall to expand the sense of windows.

2. Paint perks up a wooden cornice with color.

3. Tassels accentuate the curvy shape of a lambrequin.

4. A scarf swag can be installed above the frame of glass doors.

5. A formal swagged valance over draperies makes small windows more decorative.

6. Striped and swagged fabric looks bold but can be challenging to match.

7. A cornice can be used over glass doors to change their proportions in a room with tall ceilings.

8. Valances reinforce the shape of windows.

CHAPTER 8

FINESSE WITH FABRIC

FABRIC BASICS ■ MIXING PATTERNS ■ SELECTING A FABRIC

Fabric can evoke so many different things, depending upon its type. Certainly, brocades and tapestries are rich; velvets and wools are warm; and lace and cottons are light and airy. Whatever the fabric, it should be of good quality so that the curtain will drape smoothly, pleat well, and have more body. The more you know about how a particular fabric is made, the fiber content of its yarn, how the cloth was dyed, and whether it has been treated with a special finish will help you to select the right one for your window treatment.

For example, did you know that the weight of a fabric also contributes to the overall effect of a window treatment? Or that sheers soften the shape of the treatment and allow in light, while opaque fabrics give an arrangement form and add warmth to a room? Are you familiar with the way patterned fabrics affect the way you see the proportions of a room?

Once you start shopping for fabrics—or even ready-made curtains—consider all of these things. Purchase samples, which will only cost a few dollars. They are well worth it. After you've checked how the samples look in your home, you'll feel more confident about your choices. The guidelines in this chapter will take you through the process, step by step.

Left: **A woven-check cotton has a simple charm. You can wash it, but first check for color-fastness.**

one. A *basket weave* uses two pieces of yarn for each row in a plain-weave pattern. A *twill weave* results in a herringbone pattern. A *satin weave* has a shiny smooth surface. A *pile weave* produces loops that are then cut to create a soft surface; velvet is a good example of this weave. A *Jacquard weave* requires a special loom that can do combinations of weaves, such as plain, twill, and satin.

A design can be woven into a fabric, becoming an integral part of it. Woven designs can be seen on the reverse side of the material. Some patterns are printed onto the surface of the cloth with dye, however. The color can seep through to the back of the material, but the design is blurred. Highly detailed printed fabrics can have as many as 20 or more colors.

FABRIC BASICS

Fabric consists of fibers that are natural—such as cotton or wool—or synthetic—such as rayon. When the fibers are spun (twisted), they become yarn. During the spinning process, natural and synthetic fibers can be blended, as in a cotton-polyester mix. Yarn quality depends on how tightly it is spun, how many strands of fiber are used, and the length of the fiber. To make fabric, yarns are then woven on a loom. Yarns used lengthwise on the loom are called warp; yarns that run widthwise are called weft. The same type of yarn can be made into a number of different weaves. For example, cotton can be woven into a damask or a canvas. For a *plain weave*, the yarns are alternated over and under each other, from side to side, and from top to bottom. This is the most common type of weave. A variation on the plain weave is the *ribbed weave*, which features a thick yarn over a thinner

The colorfastness of dyes varies, an important factor with regard to window treatments. Fabric colors will fade due to constant exposure to the sun. Darker and brighter colors tend to fade faster than lighter, neutral colors. For the best resistance to sun damage, natural fibers should be vat-dyed and synthetic fibers should be solution-dyed. *Ask about the coloring process.* There are special finishes that can be applied to fabrics to help resist fading. There are also finishes to repel stains, mildew, and wrinkles, as well as fabrics with a sheen finish, such as that of glazed cotton (chintz).

A fabric's opacity influences how it will look in a room. Even if the color is dark, a sheer fabric or one with an open-weave, such as lightweight muslin, creates a soft effect and allows in light. Heavyweight fabrics, such as brocades and velvets whether they are light or dark in color, create a cozier feeling and keep out the sun.

Be aware that there is a difference between decorator fabrics and garment fabrics. Decorator fabrics have a higher thread count and are more tightly woven, so they will hold up better. Most are 54 inches wide, whereas garment fabrics are 45 inches wide. The wider the fabric, the less yardage you'll need to make your window treatment. But decorator fabrics are more costly, and so you may not notice any savings.

COMMON FABRICS FOR WINDOW COVERINGS

Textiles play an important part when it comes to delivering color, pattern, and texture to a window dressing. Here is a brief overview of some common fabrics used to fabricate curtains, draperies, and shades:

Brocade. Often a weighty fabric woven of silk, cotton, wool, or a combination. A raised, floral design in a Jacquard weave is a brocade's distinguishing feature. It is typically used for formal styles.

Cambric. A plain, tightly woven linen or cotton fabric with a sheen on one side. Curtain panels can be successfully made from cambric.

Canvas. A coarse woven-cotton material available in heavy or lighter gauges. Canvas is strong and inexpensive. It works well for shades.

Chintz. Cotton fabric, often in a floral or other all-over print, that is coated with a resin that gives it a sheen. Dry cleaning is necessary.

Cotton Duck. A cream-colored cotton that comes in various weights. It is ideal for no-sew curtains. (See Canvas.)

Crewel. Plain woven, natural-cotton fabric with wool embroidery. Dry cleaning is required.

Damask. Another Jacquard material made of cotton, silk, wool, or a combination with a satin, raised design. This fabric is widely used for draperies.

Gingham. Plain-weave cotton fabric woven in block or checked prints. Its crisp look makes gingham popular for borders and curtain panels.

Lace. Cotton or cotton-polyester-blend material featuring an openwork design. Lace is favored for café curtains.

Linen. An unusually strong fabric made from processed flax. Linen is best when used in simple designs.

Below: Understated fabrics are a good choice for a bedroom. Here, a sheer voile is paired with a light silk that drapes beautifully into soft folds when it is drawn back.

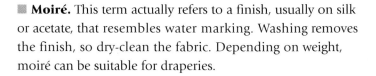

Above: Gauzy curtains made of voile have a translucency that is airy and feminine. This type of fabric looks pretty loosely draped, swagged, knotted, or twisted.

Below, left and right: Contrasting two materials, such as a heavy velvet over light organdy or a toile pattern over bamboo, adds an interesting layered look on a window.

■ **Moiré.** This term actually refers to a finish, usually on silk or acetate, that resembles water marking. Washing removes the finish, so dry-clean the fabric. Depending on weight, moiré can be suitable for draperies.

■ **Muslin.** Ranging from coarse to fine, a plain-weave cotton fabric. Muslin is also called *voile*.

■ **Organdy.** Light cotton washed in acid for a crisp finish. Organdy is used for trimmings, borders, and curtains.

■ **Satin.** A silk, linen, or cotton weave with a glossy surface and dull back, sometimes with a moiré finish. Satin is not particularly durable but is fine for draperies.

■ **Silk.** A shiny fabric made from fibers produced by silkworms. Silk is favored for swags and formal draperies.

Taffeta. A silk-and-acetate weave that appears shiny and maintains shape. Taffeta is useful for borders and curtains.

Tapestry. A heavy, woven cloth that imitates handmade tapestries.

Toile de Jouy. An eighteenth-century-designed print of pastoral scenes on cotton or linen first produced in the French town of Jouy. Toile de Jouy is used for curtains, valances, or shades.

Velvet. Soft fabric made from cotton, viscose rayon, or polyester. Velvet features a smooth, iridescent-looking pile. Finer velvets are good for draperies.

MIXING PATTERNS

Mixing patterns can be intimidating, in part because it's subject to experimentation, judgment, and "eye." Responding to this fear, manufacturers provide an abundance of coordinated fabric collections, available through in-store design services. Such collections, selected by professionals, can save you a lot of legwork and still leave scope for your own input. If you prefer to mix your own patterns, try to match the scale of the pattern to that of the area over which it is to be used. The general rule is to use large prints on the largest parts of a window treatment, such as the curtain panel; medium prints on medium pieces, such as a cornice or a valance; and small prints on accent pieces, such as borders.

To experiment with mixing patterns, start simply. Geometric patterns often mix well together—stripes with checks, plaids or dots. It is always easier to mix patterns that contain one or more common colors or have a similar level of intensity between the prints. A solid-color companion that pulls out

Above: **Silk taffeta, which is a plain-weave fabric with a crisp sheen, has the elegance and femininity of a ball gown. Here, it has an iridescent quality to it.**

a hue shared by two prints provides another connection. Exact matches are the backbone of manufacturers' coordinated collections. But to arrive at your own personal mix, you can interpret the principle loosely and experiment to see which pattern combinations work for you. Designers develop a knack for picking eye-catching combinations— and through experimentation you will, too. Look through magazines for ideas. Remember, however, that it is important to give your eyes a place to rest. Be sure to add a solid-color fabric or trimming into the mix, as well.

SELECTING A FABRIC

Finding the right fabric is a matter of trial and error. Your first choice may not drape as well as you wanted or may come in only a color that is too dark. To help the process go more smoothly, follow these steps.

ONE Develop a color scheme. Now is the time to pick a color for your window covering. You can establish it based on elements that already exist in the room—an upholstered sofa, a carpet, or even a favorite painting. Once you determine the main color for the treatment, choose an accent or two. Accent colors can be used for borders, trimmings, and even linings. (For more about color, see Chapter 3, "What's Your Decor?" page 34.) Collect samples of various fabrics, and compare the colors until you find something that you like.

TWO Choose the right type of fabric for your window treatment. For the finished result to be successful, the fabric that you choose needs to suit the window treatment. Canvas is an excellent fabric for a shade, but it is too stiff to drape as a swag. A balloon shade needs a tightly woven material so that the scallops at the hem will hold their shapes and not sag. Don't judge a fabric by its looks alone; check the weight, weave, and dyeing process, and how the fabric should be cleaned. When you are using more than one type of fabric, make sure all of the materials are compatible in terms of weight and cleaning requirements. There are several things to think about before you decide.

Durability. If you expect to have your window treatment for a long time, choosing a strong fabric is important. Some fabrics, such as silk, will fade or deteriorate easily due to sun damage. These types of materials require a lining or a special finish for protection.

Drapability. How the fabric should hang depends on the type of window treatment you want. Voile is often used for scarf swags because it is lightweight and hangs beautifully, but this sheer material may not have enough body for a pleated treatment. Thickly woven fabrics, such as tapestry, may be best suited to straight, not tieback, panels. In any case, fabric should drape gracefully into tight or loose folds.

Cleaning recommendations or requirements. This goes back to the issue of maintenance, as was discussed in Chapter 4, page 44. If you don't want to fuss with your window dressing, you need an easy-care fabric. If you don't mind investing time—and money—in the upkeep of your arrangement, you have more options.

Synthetic fabric treatments. A special finish adds to the durability of a fabric. It can provide resistance to sun damage, mildew, and stains. Some finishes give the fabric more body for better draping.

THREE Check how the fabric looks in your home. Once you've narrowed down the choices, collect fabric samples. Because a small swatch may not show a complete pattern repeat, try to get the largest sample that you can. You may be able to borrow a large swatch from the fabric store. If not, buy a yard to take home. Hang the swatches next to the window on which you're planning to use them. Take note of the fabric's opacity during the day and in the evening when the lights are on. How do the colors hold up? Colors that look good in the evening may appear washed out in daylight. At night falls, some dark colors can look muddy.

Opposite, top: Matte-finished slub silk has tiny nubs and looks like heavy linen.

Opposite, bottom: A ethnic print fabric adds an exotic touch to a room.

Right: Silk and other fabrics can be treated, today, to enhance durability.

SMARTtip   A Fabric's Drape IQ

Test a fabric's draping ability by looking at a large piece in a fabric store. Gather at least 2 to 3 yards of material, holding one end in your hand. Check how it drapes. Does it fall into folds easily? Also look at the pattern when it is gathered. Does the design become lost in the folds? Ask a salesclerk or a friend to hold the fabric and look at it from a few feet away.

a gallery of smart ideas

1 A good-quality lined cotton fabric, treated with a stain-resistant finish, is suitable for a child's room.

2 A contrasting lining offers an opportunity to mix colors, patterns, or textures.

3 A woven check or plaid fabric should be carefully matched so that the pattern lines up evenly on a window.

4 The right fabric can soften the look of a window without obscuring a view.

5 Chenille draperies with a cut pile resemble cut velvet.

6 Spicy silk tones blend beautifully with the warm woodwork in this room.

7 White lace that has been lined with green silk offers subtle color under the pattern.

5

6

7

TASSELS AND TRIMMINGS

FINISHING TOUCHES THAT ADD FLAIR ■ TIEBACKS ■ RUFFLES AND BORDERS ■ TASSELS ■ CHOUX AND ROSETTES ■ TRIMMINGS

Once the basic curtain design is established, that's your cue to make the arrangement truly your own. The decorative embellishments that you select to accent the window decor reflect your personality and can give your design an individuality as unique as your own.

Decorative embellishments come in many forms. *Passementerie*—the French term for tassels and trimmings—encompasses a whole range of beautiful interlaced, braided, and fringed decorations that have traditionally been used to enhance window decor. Peaking during the Victorian era, passementerie has recently made a comeback—although now it is used with the refinement of the twenty-first century and not the excessiveness of the nineteenth century.

Other accessories for curtains include tiebacks, borders, rosettes, and choux. The decorative potential of tiebacks is often taken for granted. Whether it is pleated, shaped, tied, or knotted, a tieback adds color and ornament to a treatment, as well as influencing its profile. Ruffled borders have always been consistently popular; appliquéd borders are a way of adding a custom motif to a drapery design. Rosettes and choux, in all their many forms, punctuate swags, scarves, valances, and even tiebacks.

SMART steps

ONE Choose a color. Tiebacks, ruffles, rosettes, and choux tend to be made from the same material as the curtain, but borders, tassels, and trimmings can complement or contrast the color of the face fabric. By choosing embellishments that subtly complement your window decor, you can enhance the entire effect. With patterned fabric, pull out a complementary hue from the design. With solid colors, try going one shade deeper for the embellishment. Contrasting the fabric color can be trickier to get right, but the results can be eye-catching.

Take a sample of the curtain fabric with you when you shop for tassels and trimmings so that you will get the best color match or complement. Buy more than you need, not less: Should you come up short and need to purchase more, the dye from batch to batch will not match exactly. If you can't find the color that you want, some stores will custom-dye trimmings. However, many companies work with the trade (professionals) only, so you may have to purchase the embellishment through an interior designer.

TWO Check the workmanship on tassels and trimmings. Passementerie varies in quality—and in price. It can range from $2 to over $70 dollars for a tassel. Why is there such difference in price? It depends on whether the tassels and trimming are made by hand or machine. The type of thread used—such as silk, linen, viscose, cotton—also influences the cost. All passementerie should be evenly dyed and consistently smooth in appearance. When buying high-quality tassels, look for hand-tied pieces without any glue. Trimmings should not have

FINISHING TOUCHES THAT ADD FLAIR

No window treatment is truly complete without embellishments. These decorations accent notable features, create intriguing profiles, and inject extra color into any arrangement. How do you pick the right ornament for your window decor? Follow these easy steps.

loose threads along the top and bottom edges or breaks in the lengths.

THREE Think about scale and proportion. As was discussed in Chapter 2, page 20, scale and proportion are integral elements in designing a window treatment. This is no less true when choosing decorative embellishments. A 4-inch-wide flat braid may overwhelm a café curtain, but a ½-inch border of ribbon may give it panache. Conversely, a rosette that is too small will look insignificant on an elaborate pleated-and-gathered valance. Trimmings and borders can emphasize an element by giving it visual weight. Bullion fringe will call attention to the conical shape of a pipe tail so that it doesn't go unnoticed on the swag.

FOUR Remember—less is more. It is easy to overdo decorative embellishments. The point of these accessories is to enhance the window treatment, not overshadow it. If you are designing a formal arrangement, you want the effect to be sumptuous. Tasseled tiebacks on the panels and silk cording on the valance may look elegant; double-ruffles and tasseled tiebacks on the panels and rosettes, silk cording, and fan-edge fringe on the valance may be too busy, ruining the overall impression. If you prefer informal window dressings, keep embellishments to a minimum—one or two, at the most. For instance, if you are using prairie points on your shade, let that decoration stand alone. Add ornamentation slowly and sparingly. An economical way to test your choice is to make a quick sketch of the window treatment.

Opposite: A goldtone metal tassel adds emphasis to the points in a pointed swag valance. Small curtain ornaments can be purchased or fashioned from found objects.

Below: A looped fringe dresses up the hem of this curtain's attached valance. The length of the fringe was chosen to keep the trimming in proportion to the valance.

Tiebacks

Most window treatments look best when gracefully draped. Tiebacks are strips of fabric that gently hold back a curtain panel, giving it form and establishing the final shape of the arrangement. They also provide the opportunity to show off a window dressing's contrast lining.

Traditionally, tiebacks were made from fabric, ribbons, or rope with tassels. (For more information about tasseled tiebacks, see page 139 in this chapter.) But tiebacks can be successfully fabricated from such imaginative materials as ribbon-covered hairclips, strings of beads, scarves, and belts.

To hang tiebacks, attach a small hook to the wall at the appropriate height. (Other options include using ornate holdbacks and concealed-tieback holders; see Chapter 10, "Designer Hardware," on page 156.) Sew metal rings or fabric

Bow Tieback

Knotted Tieback

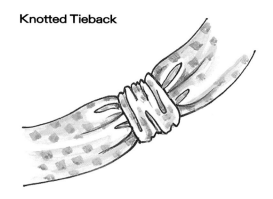

Braided Tieback

Left: You can play with the position of curtain tiebacks until they look right. A good rule of thumb is to place tiebacks slightly below or above center.

Pleated Tieback

Ruffled Tieback

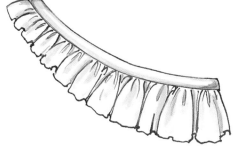

Crescent Tieback

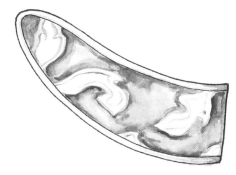

Above, right: These bow tiebacks were fashioned from strips of fabric that was used to create a pretty border along the bottom of the panels.

loops onto the ends of the tieback, and then fasten them onto the hook.

Fabric Tieback. A fabric tieback is a narrow strip of curtain material that is lined. For a bow tieback, you literally tie a strip of fabric or a ribbon in a bow onto the curtain. Or you can use a loop of fabric with a pre-made bow attached. You can position the bow toward the front, side, or back of the panel. A knotted tieback is simply tied in the center, creating a decorative but unobtrusive accessory. A braided tieback consists of three strips of fabric that are plaited. It can also be made of welting (fabric-covered cording) for a fuller, puffier effect.

You can fashion a tieback from pencil pleats, too. Make sure to have a buckram backing so that the pleats hold their shape. You can also trim fabric tieback with a ruffle.

Shaped Tieback. Shaped tiebacks are formal, and sometimes considered dated. A template is used to establish the basic shape of the tieback. Some typical shapes are crescents, scallops, and rectangles with round corners. A shaped tieback is stiffened by a buckram backing. Although a shaped tieback is usually made to match the curtain fabric, it can be adorned with piping, rosettes, or buttons.

Ruffles and Borders

Ruffles and borders are attractive ways to finish off the edge of a curtain or the hem of a shade. Like other embellishments, these edgings add definition to a treatment's shape.

Prairie Points. Prarie Points are small squares of material placed at an angle to the edge of the curtain fabric, resulting in a zigzag border.

Ruffles. A ruffle is a border of gathered fabric attached to the edge of a curtain or shade. A double ruffle features two layers of frill. A pleated ruffle falls in neat folds.

Borders. A border can be as simple as an attractive ribbon, a braid, or a piece of contrasting fabric attached to the edge of a treatment. Appliquéd borders are cutout patterns sewn onto the edge of a curtain or shade. Some of the motifs include waves, leaves, Greek key patterns, and geometric designs.

Above: A simple border emphasizes the shape of the valance on the shades.

Prairie Points

Ruffle

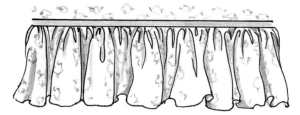

Pleated Ruffle

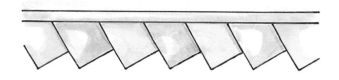

Double Ruffle

Appliquéd Border

Tassels

The tassel is the purist form of decoration for decoration's sake. Consisting of a head and a skirt, a tassel is typically made of silk, cotton, linen, or wool. Other materials, such as jute or beading, are also used.

The tassel's head is constructed from a wooden form or bead covered with thread and tatting (a lace of looped and knotted thread). Flat, dome, ball, arrow, or rectangular forms can be used to shape the head. The skirt extends below the head and can be made of bullion fringe or cut or looped yarn.

A dangling tassel draws the eye to whatever feature it is accenting. It is often centered on a valance or a swag; it can also punctuate the notches of a cornice. A tassel can be a visual counterbalance to the long tail of an asymmetrical treatment. Or it can function as a shade pull. When you attach a tassel to a thick cord, it becomes a luxurious tieback.

Frog Tassel

Key Tassel. The traditional key tassel was originally used on key fobs.

Rosette. In this case, the rosette is a circular ornament of tatting, painted wood, or semi-precious stone baubles with a tassel attached.

Frog Tassel. Made of three loops of cording with a rosette in the center, the tassels hang from cording behind the rosette.

Below: A tasseled border adds a rich finishing touch to curtains.

Beaded Tassel

Choux and Rosettes

Choux and rosettes usually adorn multi-layered window dressings and swags, but they also embellish tiebacks. These decorations highlight any spot on which they are placed, so choose their location wisely.

Choux. A choux projects out farther than other finishing touches, so it is more noticeable. With a small piece of buckram as a backing, a circle of fabric is gathered and secured randomly, creating a ruched ball. For scarves, there is an easier and less formal way to make a choux: the fabric is knotted.

Maltese Cross. Made of curtain fabric or ribbon, a Maltese Cross consists of four loops and no tails. The center of the cross is disguised by a small circle of material or a fabric-covered button. This bow is a somewhat informal decoration.

Fabric Rose. Often made with wire ribbon, the material is gathered and secured from the center outward, creating a spiral of fabric.

Ruffle Rosette. The flower-like embellishment of a ruffle rosette features a tightly gathered center with a ruffled edge.

Knife-Pleated Rosette. For the tailored effect of a knife-pleated rosette, the material is pleated and the ends are joined to make a circle. A fabric-covered disc is attached to the center of the rosette.

Above, right: A ruffle rosette that is attached to the valance at the corner hides the place where the valance is attached to the wall.

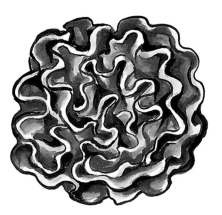

Choux

Maltese Cross

Fabric Rose

Ruffle Rosette

Knife-Pleated Rosette

Above: A knotted rosette or choux can add an expensive look to window treatments.

Trimmings

Trimmings cover a variety of border-like edgings that are used to embellish curtains. This category encompasses gimps, braids, picot braids, piping, cording, jacquard borders, and fringes. Originally designed to cover seams and edges, these borders add definition to the shape of a treatment. For instance, the edge of a cascade jabot can be highlighted by fringe.

Trimmings are woven from fibers, such as wool, silk, cotton, or gold or silver threads. They can also be fabricated from other less-typical materials, such as chenille, organdy, or hemp. Fringes, in particular, can feature beading, feathers, or stone baubles, which can sometimes glimmer as they capture a hint of sunlight or produce a soft chiming effect as they move in the breeze.

Picot Braid. The flat picot braid has a pattern of small loops or scallops projecting from the side of the border.

Gimp. Gimp is a ribbon-like braid of silk or cotton that is stiffened with a wire.

Flat Braid. Also known as a galloon, flat braid can be woven in any fiber. It ranges in size from 1 1/2 to 3 inches wide.

Cording. Yarn is twisted together to make a cord. Thick cording is used for tiebacks with tassels.

Jacquard Border. A flat border woven on a Jacquard loom, Jacquard border can be 2 1/2 to 6 inches wide.

Fan-Edge Braid. Fan braid has small looped cords in an undulating pattern.

Piping. Also called welting, piping is a strip of fabric folded over a cord. Although it is available ready-made, it can be sewn by hand.

Fringe. With a skirt of twisted cords, fringe can be topped by a braid, lace, or crochet-work heading. The skirt can be ornamented by tassels, teardrops (fabric-covered balls), tufting (a cluster of threads), and beading. Brush fringe has a row of cut cords. Originally made of gold or silver thread, bullion fringe features thick, twisted cords. Campaign fringe has one or more rows of bell-shaped tassels; its name comes from the Italian word campana, meaning bell. Tasseled fringe ties together sections of the cord at even intervals. Looped fringe leaves the twisted cords uncut.

Above: You can think of tassels, dangling fringe, and other trimmings as jewelry for window treatments.

Picot Braid

Flat Braid

Cording with Selvage

Jacquard Border

Above: A cord or braid attached to the outside hem of a curtain can pick up an accent color from a print in the curtain or some other soft furnishing.

Fan-Edge Braid

Brush Fringe

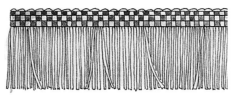

Bullion Fringe

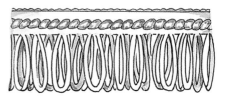

Campaign Fringe

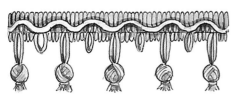

Tasseled Fringe

Looped Fringe

1

3

a gallery of...

4

2

1 Add unique trimmings to a tieback.

2 Everyday ribbon can serve as a pretty tieback.

3 Glass knobs can be functional as well as decorative.

4 Red bandanas reinforce this room's theme.

5 Hot-glue or hand-stitch rickrack and buttons to fabric remnants to make a colorful tieback.

6 Campaign fringe is subtly decorative on a kitchen shade.

7 A tortoise-embellished cuff tieback looks playful.

8 Alternating colors of tassel fringe on the valance coordinate with the check fabric.

...smart ideas

1 Banding an edge with a contrasting strip of fabric adds a tailored look.

2 Tassels help to shape the soft folds of jabots.

3 A rope-and-tassel tieback looks elegant with a heavy brocade fabric.

4 Trimmings are typical of formal, period styles.

5 Rosettes draw attention to the top of a window treatment.

6 A ruffled heading adds more interest to panels.

DESIGNER HARDWARE

**CHOOSING HARDWARE ▪ CURTAIN RODS ▪
POLES AND FINIALS ▪ HOLDBACKS ▪
OTHER HARDWARE**

These days, window-treatment hardware extends far beyond the standard traverse rod or basic pole. Although some supports are intended to remain unseen, allowing the curtains to draw all the attention, other types are meant to be part of the spotlight. You can order custom designs, in materials and finishes to match your decor, but you can also find many fine choices in stores. Moreover, you can find style in all price ranges.

Finials, holdbacks, drapery pins, and swag holders come in an endless array of motifs—from suns and fleurs-de-lis to curlicues and ram's heads. Even rods and poles have decorative possibilities. They are available in a variety of materials, including metals (brass, cast and wrought iron, steel, and gold- and nickel-plated metal), plastic, and wood. Faux finishes, such as verdigris and marbling, are also favorite ways to customize fittings.

If your drapery hardware will be visible, you can choose a style that complements the curtain's design, but contrasting it can be equally effective. For instance, if the treatment is a tabbed curtain in a sheer fabric, you can play against the delicacy of the fabric by choosing a narrow, wrought-iron pole with a shepherd's crook finial.

ware. However, when a window is poorly located, there are exceptions. A window that is too close to the ceiling requires ceiling-mounted hardware. Corner windows or a window close to a corner are other problem spots. Stay clear of using a pole that has large, ornate finials, because it will be too large for these situations. Instead, use an expandable traverse rod for curtains or swag holders for scarves because they require less space.

Is the treatment stationary? Or is it movable? Again, the hardware should suit the situation. For a stationary treatment, try a continental rod or a pole with finials. *Traverse rods* are the best for movable treatments. You can decide between a one-way or a two-way draw. A one-way draw pulls the curtain in one direction—either right or left. A two-way type draws the panels in opposite directions. The *headrail* anchors a shade or a blind, and it is the location for the track (if there is one). Vertical blinds can be drawn to one side or can split in the middle. The latter is known as a *split headrail* because, like a two-

CHOOSING HARDWARE

Before you can choose your hardware, you have to evaluate your window and the window decor that you're planning to use. Will the treatment be installed inside or outside the window frame? Each situation calls for a different type of drapery hardware. An inside mount needs a rod or a pole that fits within the frame of the window. Suggestions include a basic traverse rod, a ceiling-mounted rod, a swivel rod, and a tension rod. There are no restrictions with an outside mount, so you can use any style of drapery hard-

way traverse rod, each half of the treatment moves in a different direction. A two-on-one headrail features two cellular shades on one headrail, which is ideal for wide windows or sliding glass doors.

Will the hardware be seen? Or will it remain hidden? This also influences your choices. When the hardware will be shown off, a pole with finials is the most decorative option. But if your design requires easy operation, a concealed-track rod may work for you. If the hardware will remain unseen, go with a traverse rod. It will allow you to move the curtain easily and can be tucked away under a valance or cornice.

OPERATING CONTROLS

There are different types of operating controls for window treatments. A *cording system* is the most common means of moving a treatment, but it varies with the style of the window decor. For instance, a cord pulley on a traverse rod draws curtains aside. For some shades, a system of rings and cords pulls the fabric up and down. In the case of vertical blinds, a chain system with a wheel mechanism moves the slats from side to side, as well as adjusts their angle. For any of these, you can choose on which side of the treatment to hang the cording system.

A wand is another way to draw window dressings, particularly vertical blinds. Basically, it's a plastic pole that hangs from one side of an arrangement, in place of the cording. When drawn by hand, the wand pushes the treatment along the track. When the wand for vertical blinds is twisted, it rotates the slats to any angle you desire.

Plan ahead where you want the operating controls to be located. In general, put an operating control on the side where you have the best access and where it is the least visible. If there is a cording system and a wand, keep both controls on the same side of the treatment. Operating controls for corner windows will look cluttered if you put them in the middle. Place the cording system or wands on the left for the left window and on the right for the right unit.

Opposite: Although the rod's finial is large, it can extend beyond the wall of this window bay.

Right: Tabs that are attached to this valance are held up by ball finials that have been screwed into the wall.

SMARTtip   BRACKETS

Although it is rarely noticed, a bracket plays an important role in supporting rods and poles. If a treatment rubs against a window frame, an extension bracket solves the problem. It projects from the wall at an adjustable length, providing enough clearance. A hold-down bracket anchors a cellular shade or a blind to the bottom of a door, preventing the treatment from moving when the door is opened or closed.

Curtain Rods

Expandable Traverse Rod

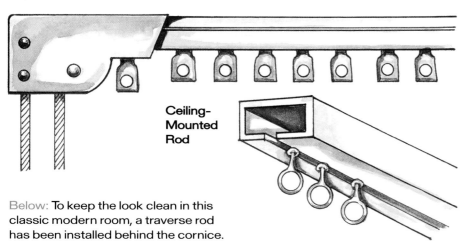

Ceiling-Mounted Rod

Below: To keep the look clean in this classic modern room, a traverse rod has been installed behind the cornice.

A curtain rod is the most functional means of supporting a window dressing. Because a curtain rod features a track system, it is the easiest type of drapery hardware to operate. The system consists of plastic or brass runners that glide along the track. Brackets are attached to the wall to hold the track (unless it is ceiling mounted). Usually, a cord pulley adjusts the runners, but some are moved by hand. If a rod is utilitarian and the curtain's heading doesn't have to be seen, the hardware can be installed out of view, typically behind a valance or cornice.

Tension Rod. A rubber-tipped rod with a spring mechanism that holds it in place within the window frame, a tension rod is useful for recessed windows. Lightweight curtains are the only option.

Standard Traverse Rod. There are two types of traverse rod: a basic track and an expandable version. A traverse rod is concealed when the curtains are closed. It is available with a one-way and two-way draw. This rod can be bent by a professional for a bow window installation.

Ceiling-Mounted Rod. Instead of having brackets, a ceiling rod attaches to the ceiling or underneath the top of the window frame. It works well in a tight space, such as a dormer window.

Continental Rod. Stationary and $2^{1}/_{2}$ to $4^{1}/_{2}$ inches wide, a continental rod creates a deep heading on rod-pocket curtains, giving them visual interest. A continental rod is also used to make a rod sleeve more valance-like.

Double-Track Rod

Swivel Rod

Track-and-Valance Rod

Below: When you want to keep the focus on the fabric, chose hardware that is functional and out of sight. This treatment uses a double-track rod.

Concealed-Track Rod. A concealed-track rod is a hybrid between a rod and a pole. The front is a semicircular shape that looks like a pole; in back, there is a hidden track with a cording system.

Double-Track Rod. With two tracks for inner and outer curtains, each track has its own cord pulley in a double-track rod. A triple-track version, for two curtains and a valance, is also available.

Track-and-Valance Rod. Hanging a curtain and a valance on the same fitting, a rail for the stationary valance projects in front of a traverse rod for the drapery.

Swivel Rod. Handy where there is no stack-back space, a swivel rod is hinged so that it swings away from the window when opened. It works best on small windows, particularly recessed ones.

Wire Rod. A wire rod consists of metal wire threaded through small brackets. It can be easily used for bow, bay, and corner windows. Choose mid- to light-weight treatments, not heavy ones.

Poles and Finials

Because of its decorative nature, a pole with finials can command as much attention as a window dressing. A pole is fixed to a window by brackets. (Use sockets for inside mounts.) Unless it's a tabbed or rod-pocket curtain, the treatment will require curtain rings or café clips to hang from the pole. These usually match the material and finish of the support. Café clips can be adorned with motifs such as stars or leaves.

Wooden Poles. The types of wood range from the inexpensive (pine and beech) to the expensive (mahogany and ebony). It can be left unfinished, stained, or painted. Finishes include metallic, verdegris, gilt, and faux marble. The pole can be turned to feature fluting (rounded grooves). To make rings glide smoothly, use silicone spray on the top of the pole.

Right: Finials often take classical shapes, such as this acorn motif that is paired with a fluted rod.

Ball Finial

Flame Finial

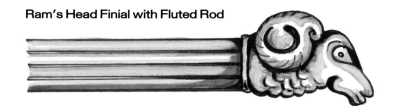

Shepherd's Crook Finial

Ram's Head Finial with Fluted Rod

Metal Poles. Brass, wrought iron, and steel are the most common metals used in metal poles. The diameter of the pole can range from narrow café style to wide cornice poles.

Finials. A decorative end to a pole, finials come in standard or custom-made motifs. They can be made of brass, copper, wrought iron, glass, ceramic, or wood. Some classic motifs for finials are scrolls, balls, shepherd's crooks, flames, ram's heads (and other animals), leaves, and arrowheads. For a creative touch, some finials can be turned into pegs for hanging curtains from the ceiling.

Above: An antiqued wrought-iron rod has a fleur-de-lis finial that pairs well with a small-print check curtain for a French-country look.

Café Clips

Ceiling-Mounted Clips

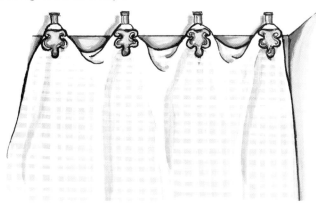

Arrowhead Finial

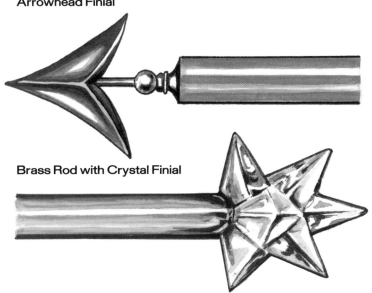

Brass Rod with Crystal Finial

Holdbacks

Holdbacks are multipurpose drapery hardware. Traditionally, a holdback is used in place of a fabric tieback. It is attached to the wall, near the edge of the window frame, and the curtain is caught behind it. For a sumptuous look, a tasseled tieback can be hooked on the holdback. When placed at the top of the window, a holdback can also function as a swag holder. Holdbacks can be made of metal, wood, or glass. Design motifs include rosettes, shells, flowers, curlicues, scrolls, and hearts. A concealed tieback holder is an adjustable plastic piece that holds the curtain away from the wall, preventing a tieback from creasing the fabric. It is not visible.

Above: A holdback can be secured into the wall or attached to the window trim. Here, a blue glass holdback accents a white lace curtain.

Basic Holdbacks

C-Shaped Holdbacks

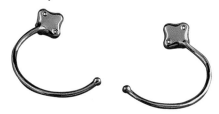

Seashell Holdbacks

Glass and Brass Holdbacks

Floral Holdbacks

Dogwood Holdbacks

Other Hardware

Drapery pins and swag holders are decorative accents for curtains. Drapery pins add detail to your window dressing. Used on lightweight curtains, the metal pins hold back a small amount of fabric. A swag holder is akin to a holdback, except with a looped piece of metal in which the swag is hung. Another type of swag holder is a resin corbel (a projecting bracket) with an opening for pulling through the fabric.

If you don't see the drapery hardware that you want or if you have your own idea, have a custom fitting made. You will need to work with an interior designer who has access to custom sources. Doing so is expensive, however.

Right: A swag holder or some other type of protruding bracket can be used to create this dramatic effect.

Drapery Pins

Resin Swag Holder

Custom Bracket

1

2

3

a gallery of

4

1 Swivel rods solve the problem of opening French doors.

2 A Venetian-inspired finish adds European flair to a finial.

3 A curved rod accommodates a bay window.

4 An iron rod with a bird finial accentuates the top of this treatment.

5 Drapery rings allow a curtain to glide effortlessly across a pole.

6 A bamboo pole coordinates the curtains with the window shades.

7 A series of metal holdbacks mounted along above the curve of the windows keep the curtains stationary.

smart ideas

C H A P T E R   11

PROBLEM SOLVING

**EXAMINING YOUR WINDOW NEEDS ■
LARGE WINDOWS ■ SPECIAL SHAPES ■
GLAZED DOORS ■ DORMER
WINDOWS ■ CORNER WINDOWS**

Even a beautiful window can be difficult to treat. In fact, the very shape, size, or location that makes a particular window pleasing may be the problem. A perfect example is any one of the variations on what are today commonly called "architectural" windows. Other windows can be equally frustrating. If a window is too tall, too short, too narrow, or too wide for the space, it can throw off all of the room's proportions. Other problems: how do you treat a small window that's tucked up high on a wall or extends all the way to the ceiling? What do you do with two windows that interesect in a corner, or ones that don't match at all?

Believe it or not, there is a way to solve each of these situations. The solution lies within the the parameters of the window itself and the basic principles of good design. The rest of the decor, your lifestyle, and your budget will play a role, as well. In the pages that follow, common problems are identified. Solutions are proposed for mismatched windows, windows in difficult locations, and other challenges, such as large sizes, special shapes, glazed doors, dormers, and corner units. And even if your situation is not addressed, our three-step decision-making process, plus the knowledge from the previous chapters, will give you the tools to turn any problem window into a decorating asset.

Left: Shutters can be custom made to fit any window. Here, they make small, almost insignificant windows figure more prominently in the architecture of the room. Plus, they open easily for ventilation and light.

SMART steps

ONE Assess the problem. Is it the shape and size of the window that is causing the problem? Some windows are visually too short and wide for a room; others are too tall and narrow. Occasionally, mismatched windows end up side by side on the same wall or on adjacent walls. This is common in many older ranch-style houses where the bedrooms have standard-size windows and small, crank-operated awning windows. Some windows are just in difficult locations because of architectural changes, such as when a room has been divided or a ceiling has been dropped. Is there a window that's too close to a wall? Or one that abuts the ceiling? Dressing large windows can also be difficult, particularly when you have two competing goals, such as privacy and light. Many of today's large homes have media/family rooms with a fireplace, a wall of windows, and no place to put the television without contending with the glare. Unusual shapes can also be difficult. Cathedral windows, Palladians, arched units, ovals, triangles, glazed doors, skylights, and dormer windows all present challenges—ones that can be compounded by the size and shape of other windows in the room.

TWO Identify your needs. With your notes from Chapter 4, review what you need from the window treatments. Is there too much light in the room? Not enough? A window treatment in lively colors can help dispel the gloom in a room that is shaded from the sun by trees or other buildings.

EXAMINING YOUR WINDOW OPTIONS

Sometimes windows are in locations that are difficult to treat. Or there may be one window that is out of place in terms of the size and style of other windows in the room.

There are many reasons why this can happen. Perhaps when the house was first built, its outside appearance took precedence over inside consistency. Or it has a new addition with windows that don't match the old ones. Or if old windows had to be replaced, local fire codes may have dictated a different size. Or an attic with dormer windows, originally intended for storage, has been transformed into an extra bedroom or a home office. All it takes is a little thought and imagination to come up with satisfying solutions.

Think about what you can see from the windows. Do you want to cover an unattractive view? Or is the view one of the reasons you moved there in the first place? Is privacy a priority? Daytime privacy? Nighttime privacy? Or both? Think about how others see your windows. Large windows should be treated in a style that is compatible with the other windows on the same elevation. This is particularly important when the window is at the front of the house where passers-by have a curbside view.

Is the window accessible? Lack of access can make cleaning a problem with a very large window or a window in a hard-to-reach location. What is your budget? Even difficult windows have more than one solution. You want to find ones that are within your budget, in terms of both initial expenditure and maintenance costs.

THREE Look for inspiration. No matter what problem you encounter, there's a window treatment that provides the desired solution. In Chapters 5, 6, and 7 (pages 56–121), you became familiar with all the elements that comprise a total window treatment. The only limit to the number of ways these elements can be combined is your imagination. But sometimes imagination needs a bit of help. You can, of course, always call in the professionals, but even if you plan to do that, it helps if you have some idea of what direction you want to

take. Study the photographs in this book; then flip through the pages of decorating magazines. Try to look beyond the curtains or shades to imagine the framework of the windows. Look for windows with the proportions, locations, or shapes that match the challenges you are facing.

Right: Fabric can be a coordinating element. Here, a window and glass doors are treated almost but not quite the same. A valance was actually draped over the bed frame in front of the window, while the door also has panels.

Mismatched Window Sizes

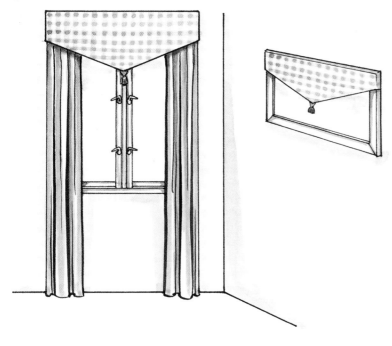

POOR PROPORTIONS

Proportion is a design element that is important to all the components of a room. When a window is too tall, too narrow, too wide, or too short, it throws off the room's entire design. Fortunately, window treatments are a fabulous way to camouflage any of these flaws without the expense and upheaval of replacing the offending window.

Tall and Narrow. Though tall windows are desirable in most cases, certain styles can run too high and appear too narrow, adding an unwanted element to your room's design. For windows that are too tall, use a cornice or a valance to visually lower the length of the opening. If your window is too narrow, extend the curtains past the window frame, covering some of the wall. With shades or blinds, choose an outside mount to make the window seem wider.

Short and Wide. Some rooms call for dramatic windows. For instance, a formal dining room may have a group of small sash windows that seem insignificant in the scheme. To visually enlarge them, run a valance or cornice above the top of the window, and extend the curtains past the window frame. For an individual window that looks too short, try the same trick—place the curtain rod high on the wall, and hang floor-length panels. Even if you are using tabbed curtains rather than a formal arrangement, the two long curtain panels draw the eye upward, offsetting the short window. If the rod is visible, make sure the hardware is attractive or the finish ties in with the decor. Wide windows require different measures. To visually reduce the width, consider a floor-length curtain in a color that matches the walls to play down the

Left: A pair of windows high on the wall in a room with a vaulted ceiling is challenging but treatable.

horizontal form. Position the curtain so that it covers part of the window. Or consider a series of Roman or cascade shades to break up the horizontal line; the effect is increased if you adjust each shade to a different level.

Skylight with Cellular Shade

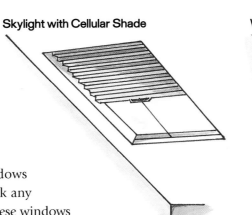

Window Close to Ceiling

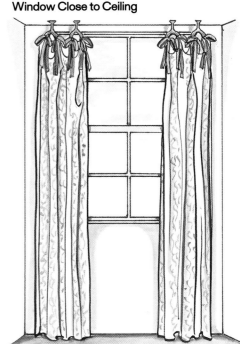

MISMATCHED WINDOWS

Mismatched windows in a room are windows unlike each other in size or shape and lack any distinctive features. The goal is to make these windows appear as similar as possible.

Mismatched Size. If the size difference is not too great, install a valance or cornice above all of the windows at the same height. This may mean mounting a heading on the wall above a window. Use an outside mount to disguise the position of the frames. Mount treatments under the header. Plan the larger window first, and then scale the treatment down for the smaller window.

Mismatched Shape. You can choose a different treatment for each window in this situation, but use the same fabrics. You can also link them by using the same hardware.

DIFFICULT LOCATIONS

Sometimes a window is situated in such a way that there is little room above or to the sides of the frame, or the window may be out of reach. Despite the location, aesthetics, privacy, or light control may necessitate some coverage.

Window Close to a Corner. When one of two windows is too close to a corner, choose a treatment that doesn't have to stack back. Blinds with a swag offer a functional yet decorative approach. Other ideas include café curtains with simple valances or sill-length tab curtains mounted inside the window frame. For a single window, consider emphasizing the asymmetry with a curtain that is tied back to one side.

Window Close to the Ceiling. Because there isn't any wall space for the rod or track hardware, use ceiling hardware, or mount a lath onto the ceiling to support the rod or track and cover it with a cornice. If you choose ceiling hardware,

the curtains will be stationary. Keep the style simple and the fabric lightweight. Or consider a cornice, which blocks the top of the window, helping to visually lower it.

Skylights. Most skylights are installed to increase light, so they are rarely covered. Sometimes, however, light is too glaring or makes the space too warm. A cellular shade with side-tracks to hold it flush against the window is a good solution. If the shade is easily reached, it can be moved by hand. Otherwise, a telescoping pole or electronic control is required.

A casual solution, which uses woven blinds, works best where there is a series of skylights. Mount the blind at the top of the skylight. Run cording down both sides of the skylight and through rings that have been attached to each end of the blind's hem. When lowered, the blind bows gently in the center, so leave enough above-head clearance.

CHALLENGING WINDOWS

Some windows present their own particular challenges because of their style or shape. The following pages explore solutions for many of these situations.

Large Windows

Today, many homes feature a large window, such as a cathedral or geometric window, or several windows grouped together, such as a bay or Palladian window, dominating a wall. These windows are often an integral part of the architectural design of a room, providing access to beautiful views and allowing a maximum amount of light. In such cases, large or grouped windows are left untreated or framed with a swag. More often, however, the placement of these windows means that neighbors can see in and that the light can be overpowering during certain times of the day. To find the best treatment for these openings, consider the following ideas.

Cathedral or Palladian Windows. A wall of windows is a common feature in a modern room, and one that can be daunting to treat. If lack of privacy is the problem, treat the lower half of a large window with curtains on a traverse or curtain rod and leave the transoms unadorned. Vertical blinds are another

Cathedral Window with Curtain

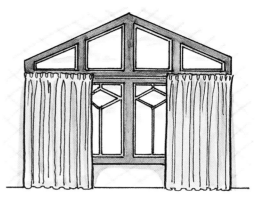

Palladian Window with Scarf

Angled Window with Shirred Curtain

Left: Shoji screens provide a translucent covering while allowing the geometry of the modern architecture to remain on view.

option, but they may look too severe for your decor. Try topping the blinds with a swag or a valance to soften the effect. Both of these arrangements show off the shape of a window while providing seclusion when needed.

Transoms. Glare from the rising or setting sun can make a room uncomfortable. If harsh light comes through transoms, you can completely cover the window with drapery. Keep in mind that treating the window in this way may overwhelm the room and look too staged. Another option is to hang a scarf across the transom, which often blocks enough light to make the room comfortable again and is less obtrusive. You can also treat each transom individually. Try shirred curtains anchored at the top and bottom of the window by rods, or vertical blinds and cellular shades in specialty shapes. A valance in a simple style, such as a chevron, can be hung on each transom. Remember, if the top half of a window is covered, usually the bottom half should also be treated to balance out the arrangement.

Bay or Bow Windows. When dealing with bay or bow windows, first decide how you want to treat them: individually or as a group. For individual treatments, try matching shades, blinds, or shutters, which create a clean, modern look. Or add tieback curtains for a softer style. A bow window requires a curved rod (which may require professional installation) or a wire hanging system. Instead of hanging curtains directly on the window frame, consider mounting the rod on the wall above the bow or bay.

Above: The windows in this room are massive, so they really need fabric to soften their appearance and bring them into scale with the rest of the furniture.

Bay Window with Curtains and Valances

Bay Window with Curtains Outside of Recess

Special Shapes

Windows with special shapes, such as ovals, ellipses, triangles, and arches, usually exist because they add architectural interest, both inside and outside of the house. Sometimes the best solution is no treatment at all. If you like the look of a bare window but sun glare is a problem, investigate professionally applied window film. This transparent covering filters out the majority of the sun's damaging ultraviolet rays while minimally darkening the glass.

Circles and Ovals. For complete coverage, stationary cellular shades are avail-

Custom Shade on a Lancet Window

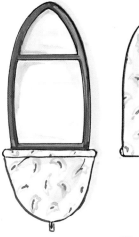 

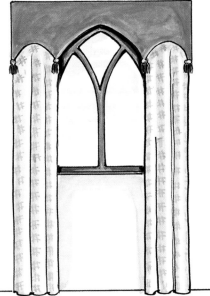

Shaped Cornice on a Lancet Window

Swag Scarf on a Circular Window

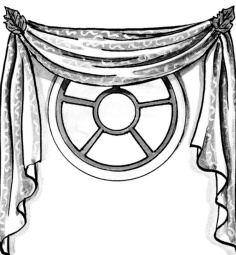

Shutters on an Eliptical Window

Sunburst Curtain on a Half-Round Window

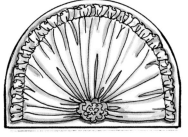

able in custom shapes. If privacy isn't an issue, a scarf swag draped over a pole or through sconces is a pleasing choice because the curve of the scarf echoes the curve of the window.

Half-rounds and Ellipses. Half-round and elliptical windows can be covered by a sunburst curtain, which is a rod-pocket curtain shirred on an arched rod. The lower edge is gathered into a rosette. Consider custom shutters and cellular shades, too.

Lancets. These Gothic-style arched windows can be difficult to treat. Try a shaped cornice with flanking curtains or specialty-shape cellular shade. A bottom-hung shade with a shaped hem is a custom item that provides maximum privacy. The shade is pulled up and attached by a tab to a peg or a hook.

Triangular Windows. Most triangular windows are left unadorned because they are usually placed above another window. However, strong sunlight can be a problem. Because of the angled shape, rod-pocket curtains are one of the few styles that work. Custom shutters, cellular shades, and vertical blinds are also attractive solutions. Remember that some of these treatments are stationary.

Round-Top Windows. You can either include or ignore the top. If you leave it untreated, you can hang any curtain, swag, valance, shade, or blind on the lower portion of the window. To cover the top, try a floor-length scarf that is gathered and secured around the curve. Or install a sunburst curtain or balloon shade.

Opposite: Mounting the curtain inside the frame allows the architectural style of the window (Gothic Revival) to stand out.

Above: Positioning the curtain poles at two different heights draws attention to the interesting center windows.

Shutters on a Triangular Window

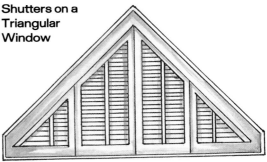

Swag Scarf on a Round-Top Window

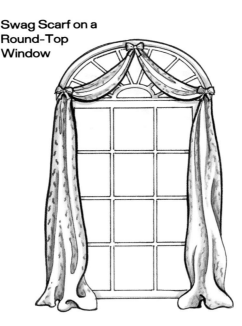

Balloon Shade on a Round-Top Window

Glazed Doors

No matter what type of glazed doors you have—French doors, sliding glass doors, or door-window combinations—the primary concern is leaving a clear passageway through the opening. If there is little wall space on either side of the opening, don't use a heavy fabric or a gathered curtain with a lot of fullness, because it is too bulky and blocks access. Instead, choose a medium- or light-weight fabric that stacks back tightly. If you are using a swag, check that it doesn't drape too low across the top where it can get caught in the door, particularly in the tracks of sliding glass doors.

Consider whether a door opens in or out. There are more design options for an outward-opening door because a curtain is less likely to block the door's operation. An inward-opening door with curtains can interfere with the movement of the door. Use treatments that can be secured above and below the glass on the door, such as some styles of shades, blinds, or shirred curtains on a pair of rods.

Above: If you don't want to install blinds or shades, metal swing brackets are a way to make curtain panels adjustable on patio doors.

Cuffed Curtains and Vertical Blinds on a Sliding Glass Door

Valance and Curtains on a Sliding Glass Door

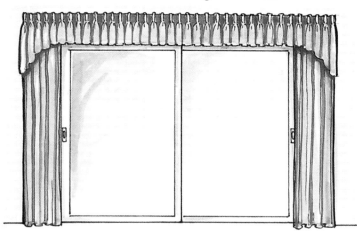

**Curtains
on a French Door**

**Shades on a
Door-Window Combination**

**Blinds and Stagecoach
Valance on a French Door**

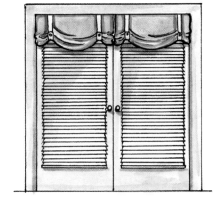

Sliding Glass Doors. Treatments that draw to one side, such as vertical blinds or curtains on a traverse rod, are the best options. Avoid any treatment that is mounted on the door itself because it will interfere with its operation.

French Doors. If the door opens out, a valance or cornice can be mounted at the top of the frame. If the door opens in and you want to install a top treatment, there has to be enough room on the wall above the door to accommodate it. A valance has to clear the top of the door. Otherwise, something that can be secured directly above and below the glass and curtains that stack back tightly work well. Shutters on tracks will require substantial stack-back space.

Door-Window Combinations. You can treat this situation as one large unit, using the same guidelines as for sliding glass doors. For example, a valance or a cornice can unify the door and windows. Or you can dress each section individually with a series of matching elements.

Above: Installing the cornice just under the crown molding makes the French doors appear to be grander than their actual size.

Dormer Windows

With dormer windows, you have the option of treating just the window itself or the area outside of the recess—or both. Swing-out poles work best for hanging curtains on dormer windows because, when light is needed, the poles swivel so that the curtain is against the wall. It's practical to use a lightweight fabric so that the hardware isn't over-loaded. If there is enough clearance, consider a roller shade. For a dormer with a sloped ceiling, such as in an attic, here is a theatrical solution: Hang a curtain rod on the wall outside of the recess, and secure the curtain with a second rod placed at the point where the ceiling and the wall meet.

Smocked Curtains with Two Rods

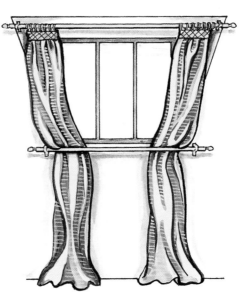

Above: An asymmetrical scarf swag gives this window in an eave authority without overdoing it.

Left: Keeping the look simple provides the necessary light filtering without obscuring pleasing architecture..

Rod-Pocket Curtains on Swivel rods

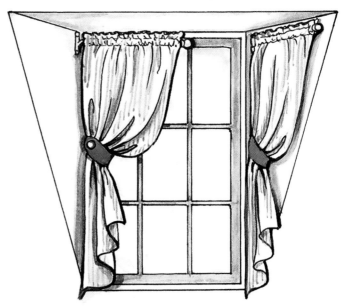

Corner Windows

When dressing corner windows, unify them with matching fabrics or a treatment that visually joins the two windows together. Pull them together with a valance or a cornice—both treatments turn corners neatly. Curtains are a good way to connect the windows, as well. There is also a variety of tieback options. The panels can be tied back-to-back, or they can mirror each other. Formal window dressings involve a combination of both styles. Try balloon or cloud shades, too. Have the shade extend past the window slightly so that the corner is visually filled in; the fullness of the treatment helps to cover any gaps. Swags and jabots also bridge the gap. Cascade tails, in particular, visually complement each other in a corner.

Balloon Shades

Curtains in "Mirror" Arrangement

**Swags and Jabots
with Tied-Back Curtains**

Above: Different sizes can appear unified nonetheless when all of the other elements, such as fabric and treatment style, are the same.

a gallery of smart ideas

1 Don't play against type. Some windows are inherently dramatic and deserve to treated as such.

2 Pelmets can offer a creative means for reshaping uninteresting windows and glass doors.

3 A collection of related objects (such as these vintage toasters) can be grouped on glass shelves within the window frame.

4 Separate windows in a bay can be treated to appear as though they are one uninterrupted expanse of glass.

5 Clever use of color and paint on the wall or ceiling can focus attention on a window.

6 A fussy design or the addition of fancy trimmings can play up an otherwise insignificant window.

7 Rich designer fabrics and hardware can make a small window appear opulent.

CURTAINS YOU CAN MAKE

MEASURING WINDOWS ▪ BASIC PANELS ▪ MAKING A MITERED CORNER ▪ ROD-POCKET CURTAINS ▪ TABBED CURTAINS ▪ A SIMPLE SCARF ▪ DECORATIVE DETAILS

Some of today's most fashionable looks for windows are relatively easy to make. Are you ready to try your hand? You could begin by making a pair of unlined curtain panels or a simple scarf valance. Gradually add some decorative details to your repertoire, such as a knotted rosette or a curtain cuff. If it's your first curtain project, choose according to your experience. Try to match it to your sewing knowledge, so whatever type of treatment you attempt, you won't feel overwhelmed. However, if you can sew a straight line with a sewing machine and know how to put in a hem using a slip stitch, you can create a variety of these decorating tricks.

Sheets are a great alternative to standard drapery fabric. Available in solid colors or in a variety of patterns, they are a fabric that's already seamed and hemmed for window treatments. Their sizes alone afford a source of material of greater widths than the average 54-inch-wide decorative fabric. Splurge on your favorite designer sheets or shop the sales for the best buys.

You can also experiment with creating some of the no-sew treatments. Seek out the various easy-to-use commercial products, such as iron-on seam tape, drapery tape, fabric glue, and pin-on and clip-on hooks.

MEASURING WINDOWS

To make your project a success, take the complete measurements of each window for which you will be making a curtain. The illustration below shows the parts of a standard double-hung window. You can refer to it as you read the instructions that follow. These instructions apply to window treatments that will be installed either outside or inside the window opening. For the most accuracy when you are mea-

suring the windows: use a sturdy, retractable metal measuring tape; ask someone to assist you; and use a step ladder, if necessary, to get the higher measurements. Be sure to double-check your figures.

INSIDE MOUNT

For a window treatment that you will install inside the window opening, there are a few simple measurements to take: the length of the window from the top of the frame to the sill, and the inside width of the window. Because some windows are not perfectly plumb, take these measurements in three spots, and then working with the narrowest measurement, round up to the nearest ⅛ inch. Do this for both the width and the length. Although this type of installation is more common for shades, blinds, or shutters, occasionally it is used for a curtain.

OUTSIDE MOUNT

Curtains, more often than shades, blinds, and shutters, are typically installed as an outside mount. Hardware such as rods, poles, and brackets are attached to the trim or wall outside the window opening. Decide where you want to install the curtain rod, and then measure the width from bracket to bracket. Add at least 3 inches to allow a center overlap. (If you are using a curved rod, add twice the number of inches the rod projects from the wall.)

Next, decide where you want the bottom of the curtain to fall: at the sill, the apron, or the floor; then measure down to that spot from the bottom of the rod, pole, or bracket. (If the curtain will hang from rings, measure from the base of the rings once they are installed on the rod or bracket.) Allow an extra 2 inches for the hardware.

BASIC PANELS

Making a basic, unlined curtain is an easy first project for someone with a modest amount of sewing skills. The materials that you'll need include fabric, fabric chalk or marker, coordinating thread, and shirring tape for a machine-stitched heading. You'll also need bent-handle shears, pins, needles, a yardstick (or a measuring tape), and a warm iron.

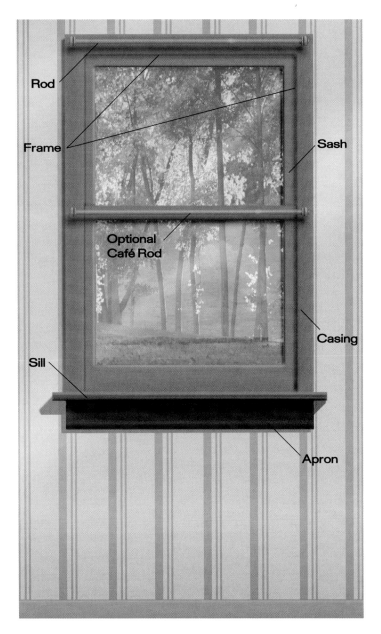

Rod

Frame

Sash

Optional
Café Rod

Casing

Sill

Apron

Trim off all selvages from fabric panels before you begin. The fabric for your curtain should measure two and a half to three times the desired finished width, plus 4 additional inches for 1-inch-wide double hems. Depending on the size of the fabric and your window, you may need more than one width (panel); you can use a partial width or even one on each side, if necessary.

Add double the desired width of the hem to the finished length of your curtain. (For example, add 2 inches for a 1-inch-wide hem.) If you're working with shirring tape, add twice the width of the shirring tape to the curtain's length.

First, mark and cut out the fabric. If there's more than one whole or partial width, lay them together, right sides facing; then join them using straight stitches. Don't forget to leave a ½-inch-wide seam allowance. Press the seams open. To clean-finish each seam allowance, place a row of zigzag stitches along each edge, or turn both seam allowances toward the seam line, and topstitch through the folded edges.

For a well-tailored look, your curtain should have neat, even hems. Pressing is an important step, as is mitering the corners. To do this, lay the fabric right side down. On both the sides and bottom, fold over half the hem allowance and press it; then fold over the other half, pressing it again. *The folded hems must be perfectly even.* Unfold the hems. Turn in each corner diagonally, folding it at the point where the inside creases of the two hems intersect. (See Figure 1.) Press the corner crease, and then fold it under itself halfway so that the point is tucked in. To reduce bulk, you could trim away this excess instead. Press it. Turn up the bottom hem twice. (See Figure 2.) Insert a small fabric weight into the hem, if desired. Turn up the side hem twice. Hand-sew (with a slip stitch) the mitered corner. Stitch both hems into place by machine or hand. (See Figure 3.) Press.

To finish the upper edge of the curtain, turn under the heading allowance once; then press. Turn under the heading allowance again. Press. Lay the heading tape a minimum of at least 1 inch down from the top edge; tuck it in at the sides, but leave the strings free. Pin the heading tape in place, and then machine-stitch it along the top and bottom edges. On one side of the heading, knot the strings, tuck them under the tape, and then stitch that side closed. Pull the loose strings at the other side of the heading until the curtain is the correct width, and then knot them. Check the width of the curtain against your window; untie the knots, if necessary, to make adjustments; and re-knot and machine-stitch the side closed.

Making a Mitered Corner

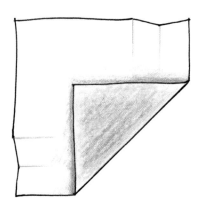

Figure 1: Turn in the corner so that its diagonal fold intersects the point where the bottom and side finished-edge creases meet.

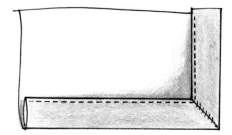

Figure 2: Turn under the corner, trimming it if necessary to reduce bulk. Turn up the bottom hem allowance twice.

Figure 3: Tuck in and smooth the edges of the mitered corner, and hand-sew it closed. Stitch the side and bottom hems in place.

Rod-Pocket Curtains

In order to make a row of gathers at the top of a rod-pocket curtain, the fabric should be two and a half times the finished curtain width. Add double the depth of the rod pocket to the length's measurement. (See "Basic Panels," page 178.) For example, if you want a 3-inch-deep pocket, add 6 inches to the length. Turn the top edge over twice, and stitch along the bottom fold. Insert the curtain rod into the pocket, and gather.

To measure for a rod-pocket curtain with a ruffle, add four times the depth of the rod pocket. That figure should be added to the length of the basic curtain panel. Turn the top edge over twice, as directed at right. This top allowance should be deeper to provide for the ruffle. Stitch into place along the bottom fold. Measure up from the bottom to the center of the heading, and stitch a second row across, creating two pockets. The top pocket becomes the ruffle; the bottom one holds the curtain rod.

Below: Contrasting fabric was used for the valance's rod pocket and at the edge of the curtain to add a nice detail.

Making a Rod-Pocket Curtain

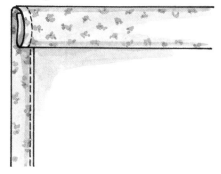

A Finished Rod-Pocket Curtain

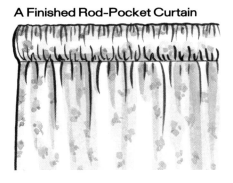

Making a Rod Pocket with Ruffle

A Finished Rod Pocket with Ruffle

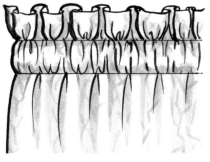

Tabbed Curtains

Tabbed curtains are a great way to show off eye-catching drapery hardware. Start with a basic curtain panel. (See page 178.) Tabs are usually spaced from 5 to 8 inches apart. Divide the width of the finished curtain by the space desired between tabs. Then add 1 to the number of tabs. For a 40-inch-wide curtain with 5 inches for tab spacing, divide 40 by 5, which equals 8. Add 1, for a total of nine tabs. For tab length, loop a measuring tape over the top of the curtain until you reach the desired length. To this length add twice the width of the curtain header plus two seam allowances. Double the desired width of the tab, and add $1/2$ inch for the seam—a 3-inch-wide tab needs $6^1/2$ inches of material.

Making the Tabs. After cutting out the tabs, fold the fabric in half with the right sides facing, and stitch along the seam. Press the seam open, and turn the tab right side out. Fold the tab in half, with the seam line facing in; then turn in the raw edges, and pin the tab at the marking on the top edge of the curtain. To secure the tab to the heading, stitch an X inside a rectangle. (See the illustration below, left.)

Other variations include bow ties and button tabs. To make a bow tie, fold a length of ribbon in half. Stitch that center point to the hem on the back of the curtain. For button tabs, follow the directions for regular tabs, as above. Hand-sew one end closed, form a buttonhole in that end, and attach the other end of the tab to the curtain. Attach buttons on the curtain at the same intervals used for the tabs.

Above: Informal or lightweight curtains can look stylish with simple tie tabs that you can make from matching fabric, ribbon, or cord.

Making a Tab Curtain

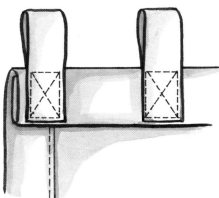

Making a Bow-Tie Heading

Making a Button Tab

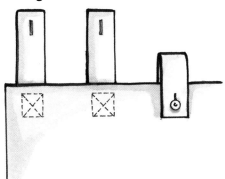

A Simple Scarf

Decide on the location of the holdbacks, and measure the distance between them. Measure how far down from the holdbacks you want the tails to fall. Add together the distance between the holdbacks plus twice the length of the tail. Add 1 inch for seam allowances. This is the cutting length of your fabric. The cutting width is the width of your fabric panel after trimming the selvages.

Based on the measurements, cut a rectangle of fabric. Fold each end in to meet at center of fabric; crease each fold. Unfold; mark a diagonal line from each upper corner down to the crease at the lower edge. Cut along these lines, and use this as a pattern for cutting out the lining. Right sides facing, sew fabrics together, leaving a small opening. Turn the fabrics right side out. Slip-stitch the opening closed; press. Fold the scarf into accordion pleats, and drape it over the holdbacks.

Above: You can make a simple scarf out of any kind of fabric. Remnants or vintage textiles can be fashioned into a chic treatment in very little time.

Making a Simple Scarf

Step 1. Cut out the fabric.

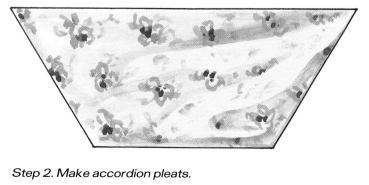

Step 2. Make accordion pleats.

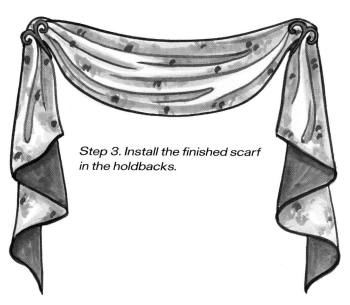

Step 3. Install the finished scarf in the holdbacks.

Decorative Details

Here are two quick projects. The first is an easy rosette detail that you can make from a short length of fabric and add to a simple scarf. The second is a cuff, used to create an attractive layered effect on tab and bow-tie curtains.

Easy Rosette: Knot a length of fabric on top of your wrist, and leave the ends hanging.

Making a Knotted Rosette

Step 1. Knot the fabric loosely.

(See Step 1.) Then tie the two ends together below your wrist, and tighten. (See Step 2.) Last, slip the material off your hand, and tighten the rosette a bit more. But don't overdo it. Leave some fullness in the rosette. (See Step 3.) Do this for each rosette. Lightweight materials, such as lace and voiles, work best for this detail.

Step 2. Tie the ends together.

Above: Rosettes can be simple decorative knots that you can do yourself.

Step 3. Fluff the rosette.

Charming Cuff: The measurement for the cuff is double its depth plus $\frac{1}{2}$ inch for the fold. For a 6-inch-deep cuff, measure 6 inches plus 6 inches plus $\frac{1}{2}$ inch for the fold, which equals $12\frac{1}{2}$ inches. Add this total to the length of the basic curtain panel. (See page 178.)

At the top of the curtain, make a $\frac{1}{2}$-inch fold, and secure. Fold the fabric down double the distance of the cuff. Then fold up half of the material. Baste the top edge of the cuff into place. Slip-stitch or machine-stitch the cuff in place; remove basting. Add tabs or bow ties. (See page 181.)

Left: A cuff adds a little fullness to the curtain's heading. It can be made of matching or contrasting fabric.

Making a Curtain Cuff

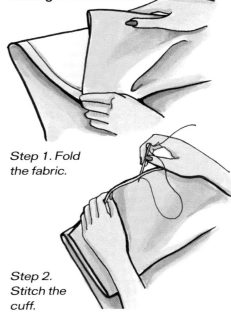

Step 1. Fold the fabric.

Step 2. Stitch the cuff.

a gallery of smart ideas

1 Grommets are an easy project for a heading.

2 Old kitchen linens can be fashioned into a 1950's-inspired valance.

3 An extra ruffle at the hemline of a valance adds a decorator touch.

4 Dress up a plain ready-made Roman shade with a strip of fabric and beads.

5 Wrap a pole with fabric.

6 Make a London shade: sew a single sill-length panel, and insert ribbons over the pole at each side to tie up the panel to your desired length.

APPENDIX

Templates are an easy way to see how different styles look on a particular window.
Simply photocopy, enlarge, or color them to try out different looks.
Mix and match until you find an arrangement that you like.

Double-Hung And Casement-Window Templates

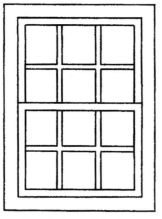

Double-hung Window

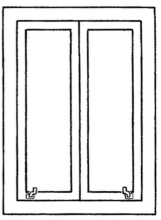

Casement Window

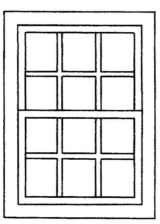

Double-hung Window

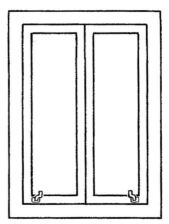

Casement Window

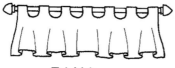

Tab Valance

Cornice

Double-Hung And Casement-Window Templates

Tapered Valance

Triple Swag

Triple Swag

Double Swag

Single Swag

Single Swag

Roman Shade

Balloon Shade

Asymmetrical Scarf

Curtain Rod

Balloon Valance

Double-Hung And Casement-Window Templates

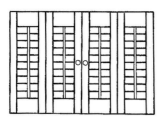

Shutters

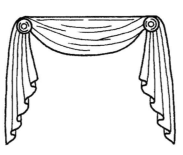

Scarf

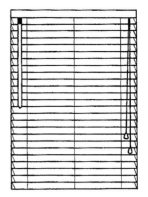

Blinds

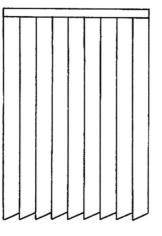

Vertical Blinds

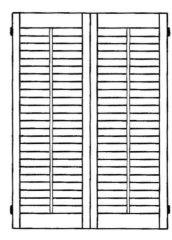

Plantation Shutters

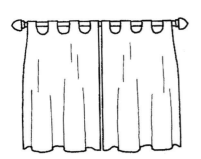

Tab Café Curtains

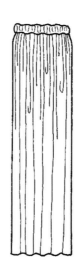

Rod-Pocket Curtains

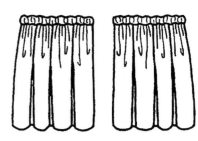

Café Curtains

Picture-Window Templates

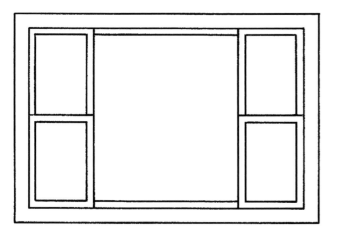

Picture Window

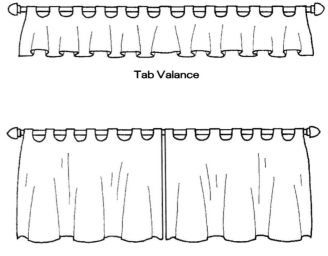

Tab Valance

Tab Café Curtains

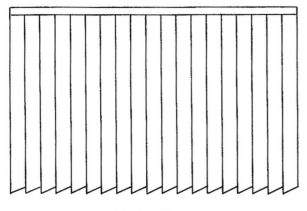

Vertical Blinds

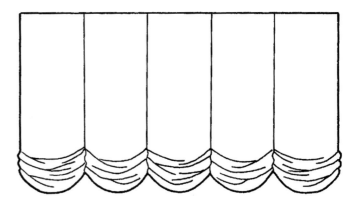

Balloon Shade

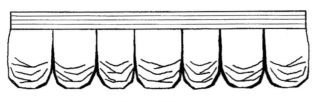

Balloon Valance

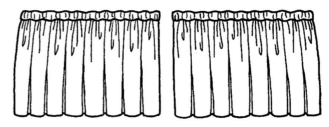

Café Curtains

Picture-Window Templates

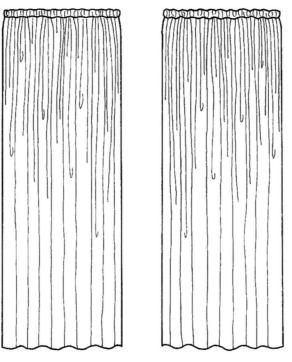

Rod-Pocket Curtains

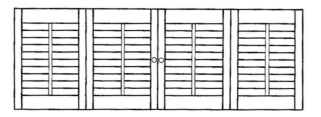

Café Shutters

Plantation Shutters

Bow-Window Templates

Bow Window

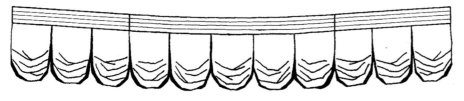

Balloon Valance

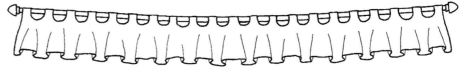

Tab Valance

Plantation Shutters

Bow-Window Templates

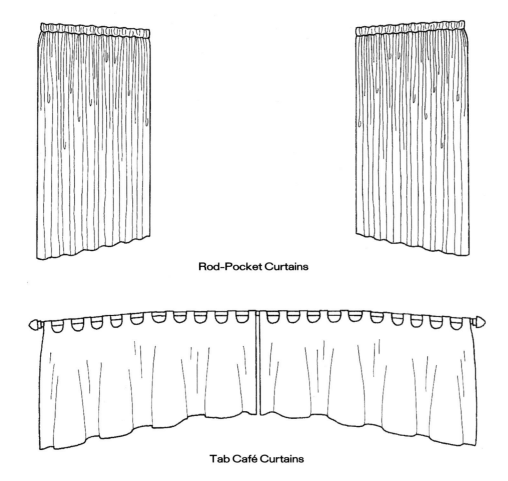

Rod-Pocket Curtains

Tab Café Curtains

Bay-Window Templates

Bay Window

Bay-Window Templates

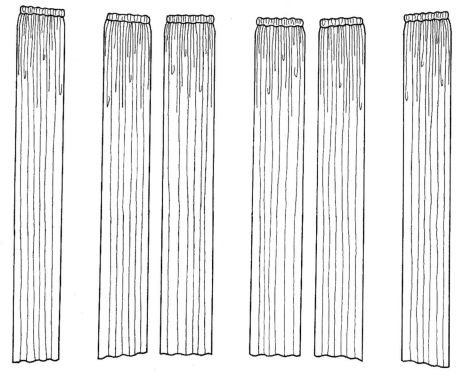

Rod-Pocket Curtains

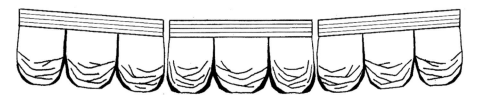

Balloon Valance

Tab Café Curtains

Bay-Window Templates

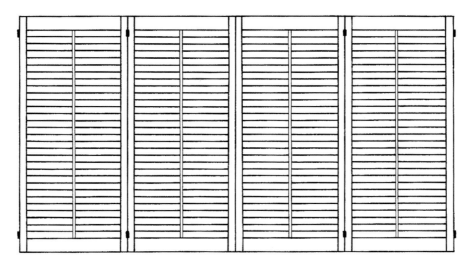

Plantation Shutters

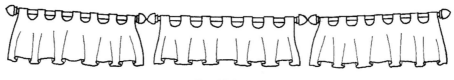

Tab Valance

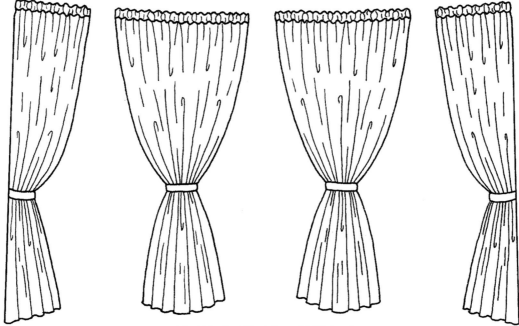

Rod-Pocket Curtains with Tiebacks

Bay-Window Templates

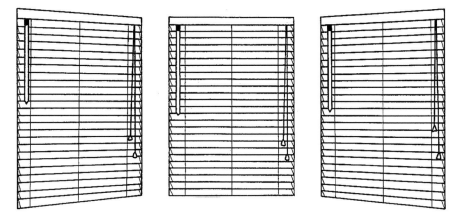

Blinds

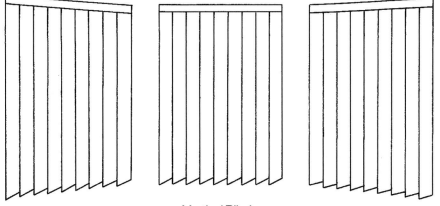

Vertical Blinds

Café Shutters

Large- and Small-Arch Templates

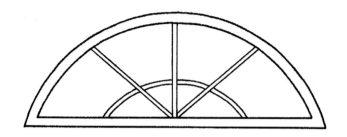

Large Arch

Large Shutter

Scarf

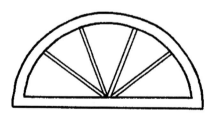

Small Arch

Small Shutter

Sunburst Curtain

Sliding-Glass-Door and French-Door Templates

Sliding Glass Door

French Door

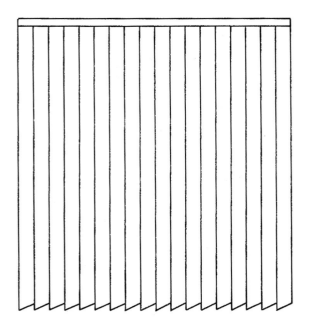

Vertical Blinds

Blinds (French Door Only)

Sliding-Glass Door, French-Door, and Cathedral-Door Templates Cont'd

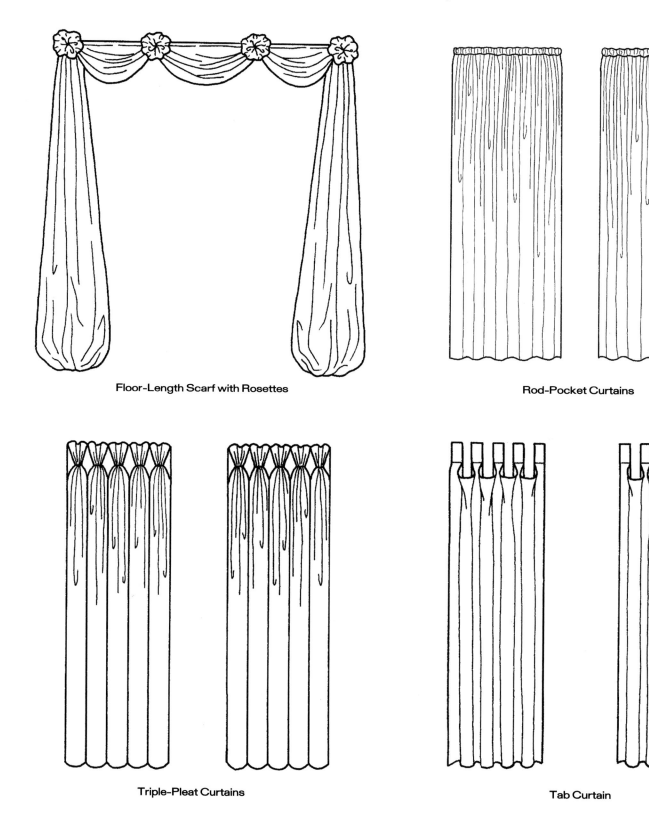

Floor-Length Scarf with Rosettes

Rod-Pocket Curtains

Triple-Pleat Curtains

Tab Curtain

Cathedral-Door Templates

Cathedral Door (left)   Cathedral Door (right)

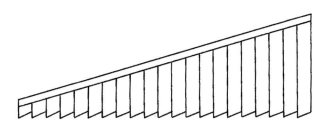 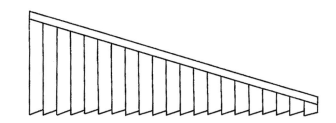

Vertical Blinds (Cathedral Doors Only)

RESOURCE GUIDE

The following list of manufacturers and associations is meant to be a general guide to additional industry and product-related sources. It is not intended as a listing of products and manufacturers represented by the photographs in this book.

American Society of Interior Designers, Inc. (ASID) *is a national organization that provides consumers with information about interior-design subjects, including design programs and continuing education. Its Web site offers a designer referral service.*
608 Massachusettes Ave., NE
Washington, DC 20002-6006
Phone: 202-546-3480
www.asid.org

Bed, Bath & Beyond *is a national retailer and on-line resource for window treatments and hardware.*
Phone: 800-462-3966
www.bedbathandbeyond.com

Brewster Wallcovering Co. *manufactures valances, borders, fabric, and wallpaper in a wide variety of styles and collections.*
67 Pacella Park Dr.
Randolph, MA 02368
Phone: 800-958-9580
www.brewp.com

Calico Corners *is a national retailer that specializes in fabric. In-store services include design consulation and custom window-treatment fabrication.*
203 Gale Lane
Kennitt Square, PA 19348
Phone: 800-213-6366
www.calicocorners.com

Comfortex Window Fashions *is a custom window-treatment manufacturer. Its product line includes sheer and pleated shades, wood shutters, and blinds. Its Web site provides company information and a store locator.*
21 Elm St.
Maplewood, NY 12189
Phone: 800-843-4151
www.comfortex.com

Country Curtains *is a national retailer and on-line source for ready-made curtains, draperies, shades, blinds, hardware , and accessories.*
At The Red Lion Inn
P. O. Box 955
Stockbridge, MA 01262
Phone: 800-456-0321
www.countrycurtains.com

Hancock Fabrics *is a national retailer and on-line source for fabrics and crafts.*
3406 W. Main St.
Tupelo, MS 38801
Phone: 877-322-7427
www.hancockfabrics.com

Home Sewing Association *provides consumers with project information, press releases, discussions, and sewing-related links.*
P.O. Box 1312
Monroeville, PA 15146
Phone: 412-372-5950
www.sewing.org

Hunter Douglas, Inc. *manufactures shades, blinds, and shutters. Its Web site directs you to designers, dealers, and installers.*
2 Park Way
Upper Saddle River, NJ 07458
Phone: 800-789-0331
www.hunterdouglas.com

Jo-Ann Fabrics and Crafts *sells fabrics, notions, patterns, and craft products nationwide.*
2361 Rosecrans Ave., Ste. 360
El Segundo, CA 90245
Phone: 800-525-4951
www.joann.com

Kirsch Window Fashions *manufactures blinds, rods, shades, and holdbacks.*
524 W. Stephenson St.
Freeport, IL 61032
Phone: 800-538-6567
www.kirsch.com

Levolor *manufactures a variety of blinds, including vertical, wood, and cordless types, as well as cellular shades.*
4110 Premier Dr.
High Point, NC 27265
Phone: 800-538-6567
www.levolor.com

Motif Designs *manufactures a coordinated line of fabrics and wallcoverings.*
20 Jones St.
New Rochelle, NY 10802
Phone: 800-431-2424
www.motif-designs.com

Plow and Hearth *sells insulated curtains, hardware, valances, sheers, and other country-living products for residential use.*
1107-C Emmet St.
Barracks Rd. Shopping Center
Charlottesville, VA 22903
Phone: 800-494-7544
www.plowhearth.com

Portsmouth Drapery Hardware Co. *manufactures fabrics and easy-to-install window hardware for residential and commercial use.*
871 Islington St.
Portsmouth, NH 03801
Phone: 603-433-4610
www.draperyhardware.com

Smith & Noble *is an on-line and paper catalog source for ready-made and semi-custom window treatments, fabric, and hardware.*
1801 California Ave.
Corona, CA 92881
Phone: 800-560-0027
www.smithandnoble.com

Spiegel *is an on-line and paper catalog source of all types of window treatments, hardware, and related embellishments.*
Spiegel Customer Satisfaction
P.O. Box 6105
Rapid City, SD 57709
Phone: 800-474-5555
www.spiegel.com

Springs Industries, Inc. *is a manufacturer of window treatments, including blinds and shutters, and is a distributor of Graber Hardware.*
P.O. Box 70
Fort Mill, SC 29716
Phone: 888-926-7888
www.springs.com

Scalamandré *manufactures and imports high-end fabrics and trimmings for the professional interior design trade.*
300 Trade Zone Dr.
Ronkonkoma, NY 11779
Phone: 800-932-4361
www.scalamandre.com

Waverly *manufacturers fabrics and ready-made curtains and accessories. Its Web site can direct you to the nearest store location.*
Phone: 800-423-5881
www.waverly.com

Window Covering Association of America *is a non-profit trade organization that represents the window-covering industry.*
WCAA National Office
3550 McKelvey Rd., Ste. 202C
Bridgeton, MO 63044-2525
Phone: 888-298-9222
www.wcaa.org

York Wallcoverings *manufactures coordinated lines of fabrics, wallpaper, and borders. Its Web site offers decorating tips and features the company's various collections.*
750 Linden Ave.
York, PA 17404
Phone: 717-846-4456
www.yorkwall.com

GLOSSARY

Austrian Shade: A fabric shade that falls in cascading scallops and is operated with a cord.

Awning Window: A hinged horizontal window that opens outward and is often operated with a crank system.

Balloon Shade: A fabric shade that falls in full blousy folds at the bottom and is operated with a cord.

Bay Window: A multiple-window unit projecting out from the exterior wall of a house, forming an angled recess inside the house.

Bow Window: A large window that is similar to a bay unit, but the recess is curved.

Box Pleats: Two folds turned toward each other, creating a flat-fronted pleat.

Brackets: Hardware attached to the window to support the curtain rod or pole.

Brocade: A weighty, typically formal fabric in silk, cotton, or wool. It is distinguished by a raised, often floral, design in a jacquard weave.

Buckram: A coarse fabric, stiffened with glue, that is used to give body and shape to curtain headings.

Cased Heading: Fabric folded over and anchored with a row of stitching to form a rod pocket.

Casement Window: A hinged vertical window that opens in or out and is often operated with a crank mechanism.

Chintz: A cotton fabric that is coated with a resin to give it a sheen.

Clerestory Window: A window set near the ceiling.

Cloud Shade: A balloon shade that has a gathered or pleated heading and is operated with a cord.

Cornice: A projecting, decorative box that is installed above a window.

Damask: A jacquard-weave material made of cotton, silk, wool, or a combination with a satin, raised design. Widely used for draperies.

Dormer Window: A window set into the front face of a dormer.

Double-Hung Window: The most common type, consisting of two sash, one atop the other, which slide up and down to open and close the window.

Draping: A technique of folding, looping, and securing fabric in graceful folds and curves. The drape of a curtain is the way it hangs.

Face Fabric: The main, outer fabric used in a window treatment.

Finial: The decorative ends of a curtain rod or pole.

Flemish Heading: A pleat that is stuffed with batting to create a puffed appearance; also called a Goblet Pleat.

Festoon Shade: A shade that is made of gathered fabric, such as an Austrian, balloon, or cloud shade.

French Door: A door, typically with 12 divided panes of glass, used alone or in pairs. It is also used as a fixed window.

Goblet Pleat: See Flemish Heading.

Heading: The horizontal area at the top of a curtain. Its style determines how a curtain hangs.

Holdback: Curtain hardware made of metal, wood, or glass. It is installed into the wall or on the window trim and is used in place of a tieback.

Interlining: Made of lightweight, opaque fabric, it is used between the curtain fabric and the lining to add body or to block light.

Jabot: In a swag-and-jabot treatment, it is the vertical element, or tail, which hangs at the side of a sweeping scallop or crescent-shape drape of fabric at the top of a window.

Jacquard: A loom, named after its inventor, that uses punched cards to weave intricate raised designs. Brocade and damask are jacquard fabrics.

Lambrequin: A painted board or stiffened fabric that surrounds the top and side of a window or a door. Historically, it also was drapery that hung from a shelf, such as a mantel.

Lining: An underlayer of fabric that is added to a curtain for extra body and to filter light and air.

Miter: A sewing technique for creating a flat corner where two hemmed edges of fabric meet.

Moiré: A fabric finish on silk or acetate, intended to resemble water marking.

Muslin: A plain-weave cotton; also called voile.

Pattern Matching: To align a repeating pattern when joining together two pieces of fabric.

Piping: An edging made of cording encased in bias-cut fabric.

Pleater Hooks: Metal hooks that are inserted into pleating tape to create pleats in a curtain heading.

Pleating Tape: A cotton or nylon strip, with drawstrings, that is sewn onto the back of the heading to make pleats.

Roller Shade: A fabric or vinyl shade that is attached to a spring-loaded roller.

Roman Shade: A fabric shade that falls into flat horizontal folds. It is raised by a cord system.

Stack-Back: The space along the sides of a window taken up by a curtain when it is drawn back.

Swag: A sweeping scallop or crescent-shape drape of fabric at the top of a window. In a swag-and-jabot treatment, it is the center element that is flanked by one or a set of tails (jabots).

Taffeta: A silk-and-acetate weave that appears shiny and maintains shape. It is used for formal-style curtains, draperies, and shades.

Tail: See Jabot.

Tieback: A fabric strip or cord used to hold curtains open; also a style of curtain.

Toile de Jouy: An eighteenth-century design of pastoral, allegorical, or romantic scenes printed in one color (red or blue) on cotton or linen. It is named for the French town where it orginated, Jouy. Today, toile is reproduced in numerous colors and on various fabrics.

Traverse Rod: A rod from which curtains are hung that features a track system or runners.

Valance: A short length of fabric that hangs along the top of a window, with or without a curtain underneath.

Voile: See Muslin.

INDEX

PHOTO CREDITS

page 1: Melabee M Miller, designer: Virginia W. Smith Interiors **page 2:** Anne Gummerson, designer: Jane Glick/Swan Hall Associates **page 6:** Mark Lohman **page 8:** Anne Gummerson, designer: Sandy Glover **page 9:** *left* Holly Stickley, designer: Ann Sacks Tile and Stone; *right* Anne Gummerson, designer: E.I. Design, Inc. **page 10:** *left* Brad Simmons; *right* Phillip Ennis, designer: Fran Murphy and Associates **page 11:** Brad Simmons **page 12:** Mark Lohman **page 13:** *top* courtesy of Hunter Douglas; *center* Mark Lohman; *bottom* Mark Samu **pages 14 and 15:** Mark Lohman **page 16:** *top left* www.davidduncanlivingston.com; *bottom right* Tria Giovan, designer: Suzanne Rheinstein **page 17:** www.davidduncanlivingston.com **pages 18 and 19:** Mark Lohman **page 20:** *top left* Mark Lohman; *top right* www.davidduncanlivingston.com; *bottom right* Brad Simmons; *bottom center* www.davidduncanlivingston.com; *bottom left* Jessie Walker **page 21:** *top* Melabee M Miller, designer: Helene Troum; *bottom right* Brian Vanden Brink, architects: Mark Hutker and Associates; *bottom left* Mark Lohman **page 22:** Mark Lohman **page 23:** courtesy of Hunter Douglas **page 24:** Mark Lohman **pages 25 and 26:** Mark Samu, page 25 designer: Anne Tarasoff Designs **page 27:** *top* Brian Vanden Brink, architect: Quinn Evans; *bottom* Mark Samu, architect: Bruce Nagle **page 28:** Mark Samu; *left* designer: Boccard/Sudell, *right* designer: Courland Design **page 29:** www.davidduncanlivingston.com **page 30:** Mark Samu, designer: Carolyn Miller **page 31:** Jessie Walker, designer: Marsha Jones **pages 32 and 33:** Brad Simmons; *center* Maggie Cole, architect: Alex Esposito, AIA, Architects; *top right & center right* Brad Simmons; *bottom right* Mark Samu, designer: Sherill Canet; *bottom left* Maggie Cole **page 34:** Mark Lohman **page 35:** *top & center* courtesy of Hunter Douglas; *bottom* Elizabeth

Whiting Associates **page 36:** www.davidduncanlivingston.com **page 37:** Jessie Walker, designer: Anna Schuster **pages 38-39:** *bottom left* Tria Giovan; *center & bottom right* Mark Lohman **page 40:** www.davidduncanlivingston.com **page 41:** Jessie Walker, designer: Eva Stefenske **page 42:** *top left* Brad Simmons; *bottom right* Mark Lohman; *bottom left* Jessie Walker **page 43:** *top & bottom left* Mark Lohman; *right* Jessie Walker **page 44:** Mark Lohman **page 45:** *top* Ivy Moriber Neal/Ivy D. Photography, designer: J.Capriano, Ltd.; *center & bottom* courtesy of Hunter Douglas **page 46:** Mark Lohman **page 47:** *left* Mark Lohman; *right* www.davidduncanlivingston.com **page 48:** Jessie Walker, designer: Elinor Gordon Designs, Inc. **pages 49, 50, 51 and 52:** Mark Lohman **page 53:** Mark Samu, designer: Teri Seidman Designs **page 54:** *top* Jessie Walker; *bottom* Melabee M Miller, designer: Arlene Reilly/Bernards Decorating **page 55:** *top left* Mark Lohman; *top right and bottom right* Brian Vanden Brink, *bottom right* architects: Mark Hutker and Associates; *bottom & center left* www.davidduncanlivingston.com **page 56:** www.davidduncanlivingston.com **pages 57 and 58:** Mark Lohman **page 59:** Brian Vanden Brink **page 60:** Jessie Walker **page 61:** Tria Giovan **pages 64 and 65:** Mark Lohman **page 66:** www.davidduncanlivingston.com **page 67:** Anne Gummerson, designer: Kathy Jeske/Purple Door Interiors **page 69:** Phillip Ennis, designer: Barbara Ostrom and Associates **page 71:** www.davidduncanlivingston.com **page 72:** Mark Lohman **page 73:** Brian Vanden Brink, architect: Chris Glass **page 74:** *top left & top right* Phillip Ennis, *top right* designer: Kat Interiors, *center right* Nancy Hill, designer: Diane Burgoyne Interiors; *bottom right* Brad Simmons; *bottom center & bottom left* Phillip Ennis, *bottom*

center designer: William Stubbs, *bottom left* designer: Tufenkian Carpets; *center* Tria Giovan **page 75:** Nancy Hill, designer: Karyne Johnson **pages 76 and 77:** *top left* Phillip Ennis, designer: Florence de Dampierre; *top center* Mark Lohman; *top right* Brian Vanden Brink; *bottom right* Phillip Ennis, *right* designer: Deborah Leaman Interiors, *left* designer: Kat Interiors; *bottom left center* Nancy Hill, designer: Deborah Lipner, LTD.; *bottom left* Brian Vanden Brink, architect: Sally Weston **page 78:** www.davidduncanlivingston.com **page 79:** courtesy of Hunter Douglas **page 80:** Mark Lohman **page 83:** Phillip Ennis, designer: Samuel Botero and Associates **page 84:** Tria Giovan **page 85:** Mark Samu **pages 86 and 87:** Phillip Ennis, *left* designer: Gail Green, *right* designer: Butlers of Far Hills **page 88:** Mark Samu **page 89:** Nancy Hill, designer: Mark P. Finlay, AIA **page 90:** Phillip Ennis **page 91:** Elizabeth Whiting Associates **page 92:** Brian Vanden Brink, architect: Sally Weston **page 93:** www.davidduncanlivingston.com **page 94:** Mark Samu **page 95:** Brian Vanden Brink, architects: Elliott, Elliott, and Norelius **page 96:** *top left* Brian Vanden Brink; *top right* www.davidduncanlivingston.com; *bottom right* Jessie Walker **page 97:** *top left* Mark Lohman; *top right* Tria Giovan, designer: Marshal Watson; *bottom right* Mark Lohman; *bottom left* Mark Samu **page 98:** Jessie Walker, designer: Drury Design **page 99:** *top right* Brian Vanden Brink, architect: Mark Hutker and Associates; *bottom right* Phillip Ennis, designer: Joyce King; *bottom center, botttom left, center left, & top left* Tony Giammarino, *bottom center* designer: Maureen Klein, *bottom left* designer: Edgewood Plantation, *center left & top left* designer: Christine McCabe **page 100:** Mark Lohman **page 101:** *top* Mark Samu; *center* Jessie Walker; *bottom* Elizabeth Whiting Associates **page 102:** Jessie Walker, designer: Katie White **page**

103: Melabee M Miller, designer: Elizabeth Gillin **page 104:** Nancy Hill, designer: Diane Burgoyne Interiors **page 105:** Jessie Walker, designer: Truffles **page 106:** Phillip Ennis, designer: Phyllis Grandberg/Walls to Windows **page 107:** courtesy of Country Curtains **pages 108 and 109:** *center* Holly Stickley Photography, designer: Janet Ott; *right* Mark Lohman **page 110:** Brad Simmons **page 111:** Mark Lohman **page 112:** Tria Giovan **page 113:** Jessie Walker **pages 114 and 115:** Holly Stickley Photography, *left* designer: Kent Magionos, *right* designer: Barbara Geiger **page 116:** Jessie Walker, designer: Pamela Whitehead **page 117:** Melabee M Miller, designer: Marlene Wangenheim **page 118:** *top right* Phillip Ennis, designer: Michael Whaley Interiors, Inc.; *center right* Nancy Hill, designer: Karyne Johnson/Panache Interiors; *bottom right* Phillip Ennis, designer: Boxwood and Ivy; *bottom left & top left* Mark Samu, *top left* designer: Deidra Gatten **page 119:** *top right* Mark Samu; *bottom right* Jessie Walker; *bottom left* Melabee M Miller, designer: Jennifer Pacca Award Interiors; *top left* Jessie Walker, designer: Lana Thorstenson **page 120:** *top right* Brad Simmons, stylist: Joetta Moulden/Shelterstyle.com; *bottom right & bottom left* Holly Stickley Photography, *right* designer: Jan Arave Interiors, *left* designer: Robert Trotman; *center left* Elizabeth Whiting Associates; *top left* Brian Vanden Brink, designer: Christine Maclin, architect: Joseph Dixon **page 121:** *top* Holly Stickley Photography, designer: Thompson Design Associates; *bottom right* Phillip Ennis, designer: Fran Murphy and Associates; *bottom left* Jessie Walker **page 122:** Tria Giovan **page 123:** *top* Jessie Walker; *center* Tria Giovan; *bottom* courtesy of Country Curtains **page 124:** Elizabeth Whiting Associates **page 125:** Holly Stickley Photography, designer: Jan Arave Interiors **page 126:** *top* Elizabeth Whiting

Associates; *bottom* Mark Lohman **page 127:** www.davidduncanlivingston.com **pages 128 and 129:** Mark Samu, *top left & bottom left* designer: Sherrill Canet, *right* designer: Vanguard Showhouse 2003 **page 130:** *top left & top center* Elizabeth Whiting Associates; *top right* Phillip Ennis, designer: Sandra Oster; *bottom* Nancy Hill, designer: Stirling Design Associates **page 131:** *top right* Mark Samu; *bottom left & top left* Phillip Ennis; *bottom left* designer: Roger Designs; *top left* designer: Samuel Botero and Associates **page 132:** Phillip Ennis, designer: Maggie Cohen/Room Service Design **page 133:** *top* Tria Giovan; *center* courtesy of Hunter Douglas; *bottom* www.davidduncanlivingston.com **pages 134 and 135:** Phillip Ennis, *left* designer: Barbara Ostrom; *right* designer: Denise Balassi **page 136:** Holly Stickley Photography, designer: KL Design Group **page 137:** Brad Simmons **page 138:** Mark Lohman **page 139:** Tony Giammarino **page 140:** Jessie Walker, designer: Janice Russillo, ASID **page 141:** Mark Lohman **page 142:** Phillip Ennis, designer: Kevin McNamara **page 143** Mark Samu, designer: Deidra Gatta Designs/Vanguard Showhouse **page 144:** *top right*

Mark Samu, designer: Deidra Gatta/Vanguard Showhouse; *bottom right* Brad Simmons, stylist: Joetta Moulden/ Shelterstyle.com; *bottom left* Elizabeth Whiting Associates; *top left* Holly Stickley Photography, designer: Shirley Roggen Interiors **page 145:** *top row* Tony Giammarino, *left* designer: Mona Dworkin; *bottom* Mark Samu, designer Teri Seidman **page 146:** Mark Samu, *right* designer: Carpen House **page 147:** *top right* Mark Lohman; *bottom right & left* Mark Samu; *left:* Vanguard Showhouse 2002, *right* designer: Saratoga Signature Interiors/Vanguard Showhouse **page 148:** Tony Giammarino **page 149:** *top* courtesy of Country Curtains; *center* Brad Simmons; *bottom* courtesy of Hunter Douglas **page 150:** www.davidduncanlivingston.com **page 151:** Mark Lohman **page 152:** Nancy Hill **page 153:** www.davidduncanlivingston.com **page 154:** Maggie Cole, designer: Sandra Morgan Interiors **page 155:** Jessie Walker **page 156:** John Parsekian/CH **page 157:** Ivy Moriber Neal/Ivy D. Photography, designer: Maureen Console, ASID **page 158:** *top left* Melabee M Miller, designer: Michele Koenig, ASID/Bruchele Interiors; *top & bottom right* Phillip Ennis, *top* designer: Linda

Shockley Associates; *bottom* designer: Merilee Schemp/Design 1; *bottom right* www.davidduncanlivingston.com **page 159:** *top* www.davidduncanlivingston.com; *bottom right* Curtis Martin, designer: Merchandising East; *bottom left* Mark Lohman **page 160:** Mark Samu, designer; East End Interiors **page 161:** *top & center* courtesy of Hunter Douglas; *bottom* Elizabeth Whiting Associates **page 162:** Mark Lohman **page 163:** Brad Simmons **page 164:** Nancy Hill, designer: Sheridan Interiors **page 166:** Brian Vanden Brink, architect: Scott Simons **page 167:** Mark Samu, designer: Courland Design **page 168:** Elizabeth Whiting Associates **page 169:** Brian Vanden Brink, architect: Quinn Evans **page 170:** Brad Simmons **page 171:** Anne Gummerson, designer: Fitzsimmons Design Associates **page 172:** *top* Phillip Ennis, designer: Gail Whiting/Design Consultants; *bottom* Mark Samu, designer: Heartwood Millwork **page 173:** www.davidduncanlivingston.com **page 174:** *top* Melabee M Miller, designer: Barbara Noud; *bottom right* Tony Giammarino, designer: Candy Osdene; *bottom left* Anne Gummerson, designer: Papier Interiors and Design Group **page**

175: *top right* Anne Gummerson, designer: John Anderson/Coppermine Terrace Interiors; *bottom left* Mark Samu; *center left* Jessie Walker, designer: Rachel Samet, ASID; *top left* Mark Samu, designer: Mayone Design/Vanguard Showhouse **page 176:** Tony Giammarino, designer: Christine McCabe **page 177:** *top* Jessie Walker; *center* Brad Simmons; *bottom* Mark Samu **page 180:** Tria Giovan **page 181:** Jessie Walker **page 182:** Brad Simmons **page 183:** Tony Giammarino, designer: Hope and Glory Inn **page 184:** Brad Simmons **page 185:** *top left* Brad Simmons, designer: Cross-Keys Advertising; *top right & center right* Tony Giammarino, designer: Maureen Klein; *bottom right* Elizabeth Whiting Associates; *bottom left* Anne Gummerson; Janet Plitt/Morgan Truesdale Design

SOURCES

Photographers: Brian Vanden Brink, Camden, ME; 207-236-4035. Maggie Cole, Meriden, CT; 203-494-8763. Ivy D. Photography, Inc., North Babylon, NY; 631-254-0761. David Duncan Livingston, Mill Valley, CA; 415-269-4799. Phillip H. Ennis, Bedford, NY; 914-234-9574. Tony Giammarino, Richmond, VA; 804-320-9709. Tria Giovan, New York, NY; 212-533-6612. Anne Gummerson, Baltimore, MD; 410-276-6936. Nancy Hill, Ridgefield, CT; 203-431-7655. Mark

Lohman, Los Angeles, CA; 323-933-3357. Curtis Martin, Palisade, CO; 970-464-1427. Melabee M Miller, Hillside, NJ; 908-527-9121. John Parsekian, Bloomfield, NJ; 973-748-9717. Mark Samu, Saratoga Springs, NY; 518-581-7026. Brad Simmons, Perryville, KY; 859-332-8400. Holly Stickley, Portland, OR; 503-283-1016. Jessie Walker Associates, Glencoe, IL; 847-835-0522. Elizabeth Whiting Associates, London; +44 020 7388 2828.

Designers, Architects, and Stylists: John Anderson/Coppermine Terrace Design, Parkville, MD; 410-357-9500. J. Cipriano, Ltd., Sound Beach, NY; 631-744-7378. Maureen Console, ASID, Northport, NY; 631-757-0002. E.I. Design, Inc., Annapolis, MD; 410-268-9595. Fitzsimmons Design Associates, Inc., Annapolis, MD; 410-269-1965. Elizabeth Gillin, Westfield, NJ; 908-654-9376. Jane Glick/Swann Hall Associates; 410-576-8780. Kathy Jeske/Pur-

ple Door Interiors, Ellicott City, MD; 410-461-1983. Papier Interiors and Design Group, Timonium, MD; 410-561-0090. Janet Plitt/Morgan Truesdale Design, Stevenson, MD; 410-486-6262. Helene Troum, Warren, NJ; 908-766-5922.

Have a home decorating, improvement, or gardening project? Look for these and other fine **Creative Homeowner books** wherever books are sold.

Design advice and tips for choosing window treatments. Over 150 color photos. 128 pp., 8½"×10⅞"
BOOK #: 279445

How to work with space, color, pattern, and texture. Over 440 photos. 288 pp.; 9"×10"
BOOK #: 279672

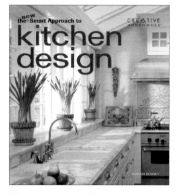

How to create a kitchen like a pro. Over 260 color photos. 208 pp.; 9"×10"
BOOK #: 279946

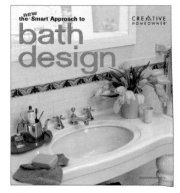

How to design a bathroom like the experts. Over 260 color photos. 208 pp.; 9"×10"
BOOK #: 279234

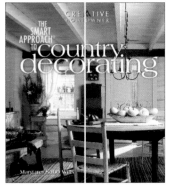

Explores new and traditional country decorating. More than 200 color photos. 176 pp.; 9"×10"
BOOK #: 279685

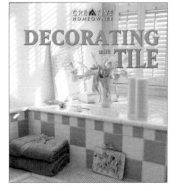

Explores the many design possibilities of tile. More than 250 color photos. 176 pp.; 9"×10"
BOOK #: 279824

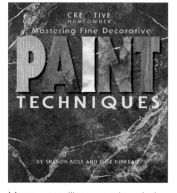

Master stenciling, sponging, glazing, marbling, and more. Over 300 illustrations. 272 pp., 9"×10"
BOOK #: 279550

Interior designer Lyn Peterson's easy-to-live-with decorating ideas. Over 300 photos. 304 pp., 9"×10"
BOOK #: 279382

Impressive guide to garden design and plant selection. More than 800 color photos. 320 pp.; 9"×10"
BOOK #: 274615

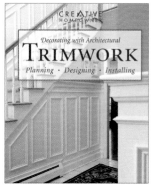

Lavishly illustrated with portraits of over 100 flowering plants; more than 500 photos. 208 pp.; 9"×10"
BOOK #: 274032

How to use moldings and trim. Over 450 full-color photos and illustrations. 208 pp.; 8½"×10⅞"
BOOK #: 277495

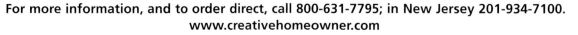

How to tile floors, walls, and more. More than 450 color photos and illustrations. 160 pp.; 8½" ×10⅞"
BOOK #: 277524

For more information, and to order direct, call 800-631-7795; in New Jersey 201-934-7100.
www.creativehomeowner.com